THE RAGE WITHIN

ANGER IN MODERN LIFE

Willard Gaylin, M.D.

SIMON AND SCHUSTER   NEW YORK

Copyright © 1984 by Pip Enterprises, Inc.
All rights reserved
including the right of reproduction
in whole or in part in any form
Published by Simon and Schuster
A Division of Simon & Schuster, Inc.
Simon & Schuster Building
Rockefeller Center
1230 Avenue of the Americas
New York, New York 10020
SIMON AND SCHUSTER and colophon are registered trademarks of
Simon & Schuster, Inc.
Designed by Eve Kirch
Manufactured in the United States of America

1   3   5   7   9   10   8   6   4   2

Library of Congress Cataloging in Publication Data
Gaylin, Willard.
The rage within.
Bibliography: p.
Includes index.
1. Anger.   I. Title.
BF575.A5G38   1984   152.4   84-13968
ISBN: 0-671-42130-1

ACKNOWLEDGMENTS

In an atmosphere like that of The Hastings Center, where ideas are constantly flowing from one member to another and intellectual concepts are scattered pell-mell through the hallways, it is almost unfair to select out some people for thanks, since all have contributed to my ideas and thinking. Nonetheless, it would be ungenerous not to mention a specific few. I am indebted to Marna Howarth, Eva Mannheimer and Eric Feldman for their help in manuscript preparation and accumulation of research data. To Carol Levine and Tom Murray for that most thankless of tasks, the reading and criticizing of impossible early drafts, my gratitude and apologies.

I am also indebted to my editor, Alice Mayhew, for her guidance in shaping this book to its final form. In addition, I am blessed with a family of amateur editors, who ruthlessly but lovingly criticized idea, content and style. Thanks, then, to my children, Ellen and Clinton Smith and Jody and Andrew Heyward.

The contribution of my wife to this book is as immeasurable as it is to all other aspects of my life. The Victorians were fond of saying that we are "authors of our own existence." She is, in every aspect, coauthor of my existence.

ACKNOWLEDGMENTS

Dedicated with love—
and gratitude for the pleasure of their company—
to David, Emily and Sarah Heyward
and Laura and Charles Smith

CONTENTS

Take me into the night where pine trees touch stars
and the movement of rivers will lull me,
for I am no wolf. I am not of wolf kind,
and only my own kind can kill me.
　　　　Osip Mandelstam
　　　　(translated by Beatrice Stillman)

1. Prologue: Mean Streets and Mean People

East 96th Street is the unofficial border that separates "the fashionable Upper East Side" of Manhattan, to the south, from Harlem, on the north. When hailing a cab to Harlem it is an unwritten street principle that you stand on the proper side of the avenue, clearly indicating the direction in which you will be traveling.

A New York taxi driver, whether he is a hired employee or a small entrepreneur operating his own cab, is licensed to operate, and thereby earn his living, by the city. One of the rules in the taxi code stipulates that the cabdriver must take his customer to any point within the city limits that the rider requests. Never mind that the driver makes more money operating in Manhattan; is lost when he enters the precincts of Brooklyn; is frightened by the prospect of a trip to Harlem at night. The rules are clear. He must go where the customer asks.

Many cabdrivers *are* frightened by trips into Harlem. While statistics will support the fact that people travel safely in Harlem all the time, those same statistics will indicate that the risks are greater in ghetto neighborhoods than in middle-class neighborhoods. For those who travel little, the statistics can be ignored. For those who travel day in and day out, week in and week out, statistics can be a threat to existence.

Some taxi drivers will refuse to go into Harlem. When the rider requests such a service the driver finds himself in double jeopardy: to take even a middle-class woman to a large public facility in Harlem may be seen as a potential risk, for as she leaves the cab, another, more threatening person may enter and direct him into an area more remote from public view, deeper into the ghetto, distant from the safety and security of public movement and public surveillance. To refuse, of course, is to run another risk, particularly if the rider is an impatient, white, middle-class commuter, who in his outrage and frustration at missing his train is more likely than others to take the time to report the cabby for his violation of the code.

Despite his trepidation the driver will usually take you wherever you ask. Once you are in the car, the power relationship shifts perceptibly; he now takes charge. The rage he feels toward you for his intimidation and "humiliation" will be manifested, either explicitly or in the manner of his driving. He can make a ten-minute cab drive up Madison Avenue an absolute hell.

To avoid such confrontation, to mitigate the constant abrasive anger that is the grit of current urban life, one masters specific maneuvers aimed at oiling the machinery; one contrives an array of prophylactic devices. One such is proper advance communication. Your signal to the cabby must indicate the maximum possible information. Since I regularly commute to my suburban home from the 125th Street station in Harlem, I understand the rules of the game and play by them.

That was precisely what I had done this particular afternoon. The cabby saw my hail while waiting for the light at 96th Street. He nodded in my direction, thereby sealing the contract between us. The light changed; he cut across two lanes of traffic from west to east on the one-way street and screeched to a stop right alongside me.

On entering the cab I picked up my copy of *The New York Times*. The newspaper is an important commuter's device. Most city-wise people accept this signal as readily as they would a "No trespass" or "Do not enter" sign. Some, however, interpret it simply as an indication that the reader is not inclined to speak. They assume their freedom to address the reader with the understanding that they may get no response. In the seven to ten minutes it takes to get from my office to the train I want no discussion. I certainly do not want argument. I have learned to be stubbornly mute. The cabdriver often prattles for his own purposes, undismayed by my lack of response. This driver was a talker.

As soon as I entered this cab I knew I was in for one standard political tirade that I am forced to endure at infrequent but not rare intervals. The major thesis is that the "fuckin niggers" have ruined the city. It is often embellished with details of having grown up "right there around the corner on 114th Street and Third Avenue," with nostalgic and romantic details of what a wonderful neighborhood it had been "just a few years ago." In my salad days, I would demur, defend, debate, leave the cab or find other means to dissociate myself from the imposed point of view; but years in the city have taught me a more effective device. I simply extinguish this oral assault from perception as I do the smells of the garbage and the sight of the graffiti.

It was obviously not the first time the cabdriver had made this presentation. That should not suggest that it was a passionless or tired replay. It was told with barely controlled rage, through clenched teeth, interspersed with expletives, gestures and all the signs of chronic anger now crystallized into hatred. I had braced myself for seven unpleasant, but not atypical, minutes of city life when chance dictated a confrontation with another example of urban rage.

Jaywalking is not a serious offense. Most New Yorkers do usually cross with the green, if only for purposes of survival. Nonetheless, the pace and urgency of the city demand that when safety allows, everyone walk—at the red, at the green and in between; it matters not. This I would call utilitarian jaywalking. The law against this particular offense is rarely enforced; one runs little risk of punishment, and the pressure of time and space is such in the city as to encourage violation.

This is a crime of convenience, not a statement of political action. There is, however, another kind of jaywalking that represents an act of defiance, whose purpose is to announce contempt for the rules. In my short daily trip between 96th and 125th streets I have seen it performed with great style. It is practiced with particular flair by adolescents. Here jaywalking is a statement. It is often a slow, mannered and leisurely saunter across Madison Avenue against the light. The jaywalker dares the oncoming driver to either hit him or else suffer the humiliation of being forced to swerve. The gesture is extraordinarily reminiscent of the casual air of the matador who asserts his ascendancy over the bull by walking slowly and disdainfully as the bull passes within inches of him at full charge. It is one of the variant urban forms of "Chicken," and as such is intended to be a statement of independence, defiance and manhood.

On this particular day one such saunterer was unaware of the nature of the raging bull he was about to meet. Sitting in the back seat, I was alerted by some change in tone or temperament in the driver. Looking up from my paper, I saw a defiant jaywalker slowly cutting across the four lanes of Madison Avenue. The actual event that I am about to describe took less time than is necessary to tell about it, but it was sufficient to raise the level of adrenaline circulating through my body and to cause me to sweat perceptibly.

The driver was on a collision course with the jaywalker. He seemed determined not to swerve but if anything, to accelerate and adjust course to ensure impact. He did not want to miss. I had visions of a dead boy hurled into the air by the taxi. The boy crossing the street became aware that his challenge was being met in a different way this time, and rose to that challenge by slowing his course. At the very moment the impact seemed inevitable, the jaywalker—finally frightened—made a quick jump out of the way of the oncoming taxi, thus saving his life. The driver let out an indecipherable articulation of sheer triumph, while the jaywalker in a rage of defeat and humiliation smashed his fist on the back of the car while screaming obscenities.

The cabdriver, now ecstatic, abandoned his routine speech, and chuckled and chortled over his triumph the rest of the way to the 125th Street station. With constraint I paid the fare and left the cab. The cabby—now in an ebullient mood—thanked me as he locked the cab doors and flicked on his off-duty sign to discourage any Harlem riders. Still unsettled, I walked to the ticket counter and asked for a ticket to Hastings. For some reason the clerk misheard me and gave me a ticket to Greystone. I said, "You made a mistake. I said Hastings, not Greystone." He answered, mean-eyed and mean-mouthed, "You asked for Greystone and you got Grey-stone." What I answered was ugly and uncivil and protected by editorial privilege. Eight minutes elapsed between my hailing the cab and my finally getting my ticket to Hastings.

What purpose was served by this anger? What was this anger about? With whom were these people angry?

The cabdriver was presumably angry with blacks. But why? And with all blacks? How is one angry with an entire population? Had he suffered some specific injury by a member of this group? Not necessarily; but even if so, how is that so generally transferable? What sustains that anger? What are its limits?

With whom was the teenage jaywalker angry? No one? Every-one? Car owners? His position, or lack of it? Was this a game? A sign of contempt, independence, manhood, pride, courage? Was he angry or bored? What private purposes were served by his defiant behavior? What are *its* limits?

What prompted the anger of the ticket clerk? How had I offended him? Did he resent me? All commuters? His work? His life? Was this his typical demeanor, or had I been the unfortunate recipient of an anger generated by an employer or a wife, displaced to a convenient and less threatening individual? And what about me? What about my anger? Here, at least, we can go beyond mere conjecture. The surliness of the clerk was surely not the "cause" of my anger. We city dwellers are inured to the minor rudenesses of urban life. Boorishness in the city, like insect and bird sounds in the country, passes unnoticed, protected from observation by its very ubiquity. My response was a final common pathway for my anger with the racism of the cabby; my disappointment in and anger with myself for tolerating it; my anger with the teenager for foolishly and recklessly risking his life and beyond all that my disgust with the degradation of public life, and my fear of some potential consequences of this social anger and the anomie it portends.

Each participant carried into each of these interchanges a set of unresolved frustrations and angers barely contained. Each may have utilized this encounter as an end point for an anger rooted in a myriad of ill-defined and trivial psychological assaults reinforced by unrecognized or uncontrollable sociological frustrations.

Modern life seems designed to generate quantities of anger while, perversely, limiting the effectiveness of the anger response. Anger, an emotion specifically engineered to protect us against physical threats to our survival, continues to be generated in conditions where the threats, even when real, are rarely physical, and even when physical are rarely resolved by our own physical responses. Our biological anger response, inbred in precivilized times to protect us against specific, identifiable, physical threats, now, when the sources of danger are symbolic, abstract and cumulative, serves only to increase our vulnerability. In becoming civilized, we have made our biologically programmed anger mechanism obsolete.

We have learned, therefore, to contain the anger response constantly generated by the multiple assaults of modern life on self-pride and self-confidence. We have trained ourselves to endure frustrations as the inevitable price of a technological society.

In this complex society we have created, we have lost control over the elements that shape our work and our pleasure. And we feel impotent and vulnerable. We are frightened and angered by signs of disorder, but even more by the recognition that what order may or may not exist seems beyond our control or design.

Beyond real misery—and surely that exists for too many—are the ever-present existential frustrations of modern life; the constant mundane humiliations; the minor indignities that corrode our self-worth. And each assault on pride and confidence increases our sense of vulnerability and generates a quantum of now useless anger. So we learn to restrict the anger mechanism, but in so doing we dangerously lower our flash point, and we suffer the physiology of a repressed and maladaptive anger.

To walk the streets of any large city is to see anger everywhere. To live in the city is to be in a state of inexplicable anger much of the time. The short fuse is a way of life in the city today, and the city today is not just New York, but Detroit, Toledo and even Middletown.[1] And the city today is a portent of a rural mood barely one pace behind. We no longer lead lives of quiet desperation. We are for the most part in a state of contained anger. What is the function, what is the utility of such anger? What possible end or purpose can it serve? Why do we need it? Does it endanger us? Can we contain it? Must we endure it?

2. Why "Feel" At All?

To understand anger, one must appreciate the role that emotions play in serving human adaptation.[1] Anger and fear are generally viewed as the two basic emotions that support our behavior in times of stress and emergency. They are part of a biological response system that has come to be "built into" each human animal by Darwinian evolution to enhance the chances of survival. They alert us to the presence of danger, and prepare us to meet that danger through mechanisms of "fight or flight." They have, until recently, been seen as basic servants of security.

But what in the behavior of the cabdriver or the jaywalker enhanced his chances of survival? How was either served by his rage? And if neither was served, of what value was that alerting and arming emotion?

Anger and fear are essential emotional resources for coping with danger shared by a broad range of animal species. When our culture conformed more closely to our animal derivations, these emotions served us well. We could attack the beast that threatened us with a force alerted and mobilized by our rage, and augmented by our intelligence. But now danger is more likely to fall out of an envelope than to jump out of a bush. Of what good is force in dealing with a pink slip, an overdue bill, a "Dear John" letter, an eviction notice, a subpoena or a draft summons? Millions of years of evolution may have been made obsolete by a mere ten thousand years of civilization. There is serious reason to view anger now as an anachronism—a vestigial, biological remnant which, like the appendix, once may have served an adaptive purpose but now is only a potential source of trouble.

Not all animals experience emotions. For a moment try to visualize what life must be like for the simplest creature on earth: the amoeba, a one-celled animal, which boasts a survival mechanism—simple as it is—that puts to shame the resources of its more complicated relatives. It is fair to assume that the amoeba is free of all emotions. It survives by indiscriminately ingesting particles around it. If that which it has ingested is nutritive, it is broken down and assimilated; if it is not, it is rejected and expelled.

As one moves up the scale of animals from the amoeba an increasingly elaborate nervous system develops. This nervous system will then allow animals to hedonically regulate their behavior via the guidance of pain and pleasure. Even the use of such terms as "pain" and "pleasure" may represent an anthropomorphic romanticizing of these lower creatures. Nonetheless, we can assume they are regulated by a mechanism which activates them in a pleasurable way toward that which is good and life-sustaining and in a painful way away from that which is survival-endangering.

It is not necessary, though one is free to do so, to see an intelligent design in this. Beyond God's hand one can simply recognize the Darwinian principle of selection: an animal may, at some time, have developed which enjoyed toxins and poisons and found nourishment disgusting; in that case such a peculiar mutation would not long have survived.[2]

It is probably reasonable to assume that pain occurs somewhat lower in the animal line than does pleasure. While pain warns of danger, it is still not an emotion. It is less than fear or rage. Pain results from immediate contact. It is therefore of limited value in avoiding danger. By the time the jaws of the alligator are on us, the perception of pain does us little good. There must be a way to *anticipate* the predator, as there must similarly be some way beyond the willy-nilly meandering of the amoeba to direct our search for nourishment.

With the emergence of the senses of smell, hearing and vision —distance receptors (as distinguished from touch and pain, which require actual contact)—animals are given a great advantage in the battle for survival. These distance receptors allow them to locate, before actual physical contact, that which is about to destroy them or be destroyed by them. They enlarge the environment; they expand awareness, and improve control over an increasingly extensive world. Distance receptors make possible anticipation. And anticipation is a giant asset in the struggle for survival.

An animal is capable of feeling fear only after it develops distance receptors, for fear is anticipation of the painful—in the broadest sense of that word—experience. But fear is not the only response to a threatening situation. Anger is the other basic emergency emotion. Whether anger actually requires distance receptors or not, it is unlikely that it developed in species with much simpler nervous systems than ours.

The feelings of fear and anger are only part of the larger emotional complex of responses which mobilize an individual for action when its survival is threatened. They are complicated physiological changes which prepare the animal for either flight from the danger or an attack on it. This concept of the fight/flight mechanism as a built-in part of the emergency response of an organism was most eloquently first expressed in the pioneering work of the American physiologist Walter B. Cannon.[3]

Emotions are accompanied by automatic involuntary responses, enacted through the means of a network called the autonomic nervous system. These physiological stress responses, which human beings share with many lower animals, prepare the body for the action about to occur, whether it is fight or flight. Pupils are dilated or constricted. Palms become sweaty. Adrenaline is pumped into the blood. Heart rate and respiration are altered. Sphincters are controlled. And blood is redirected from one part of the body to another—all this done without our will or design; all part of an automatic and rapid mechanism of emergency control.

Obviously, in addition to the autonomic responses, the *feeling* of the emotion comes through. We feel enraged, or frightened, or both. This feeling then allows us to utilize our intelligence and rationality, when available, to facilitate either the fight or the flight, or indeed to make the decision which it is to be.

A third aspect of the emotion is to transmit a warning to those about us. We are, after all, a communal animal, if not quite a herding animal. Our fear will become contagious and run through the group, warning of a common danger. But in addition, our fear or anger will be sensed, or appreciated, by the attacker, particularly if it is one of our own kind, and warn him, depending on which we signal, that either we will run and leave the field to him or, alternatively, if he wants something from us, he had better be prepared to suffer or die for it. The emergency emotions prepare not only the individual for the assault, but the group at large, and in case of an assault by one of our own kind, notify him of our intentions. In that peculiar latter sense, anger can serve to avoid conflict as well as to resolve it.

While we share the emotions of fear and anger with a host of lesser creatures, there is a wide range of emotions which are exclusively human. Some of these are almost as fundamental in their role of promoting survival as fear and rage. Certainly guilt, shame and pride—particularly as instruments or mechanisms of conscience—serve the human *species,* if not the specific human being. Conscience mechanisms direct behavior to acknowledge and conform with the human need to live in social units. Conscience ensures the survival of the community, which is ultimately necessary for the survival of any one individual. Beyond these are a whole range of smaller passions: feelings of being hurt, amused, upset, bored and the like. How do emotions work, and what are their specific functions?

The human being is in every way a unique animal.[4] He represents a glorious discontinuity in the chain of life. He is as different from his nearest relative the ape as the ape is from the amoeba. His wide range of emotions is only one way in which he differs, and this difference is related to certain other basic differences. The human animal is the least biologically "fixed," or determined, of all species. The "wisdom" of some lower forms, on closer examination, proves to be the antithesis of intelligence. The "cleverness" of the insect is exposed as stupidity when, like a computer, it collapses in the face of even small aberrations or deviations from its coding

by pathetically repeating its fixed messages and providing ans.
to questions that are no longer being asked. Human intelligence is
in many ways an alternative to fixed instincts. Intelligence is both
the instrument of and the essential for serving human autonomy.
We are allowed choice, and to use that choice wisely, we must
think, draw on experience, anticipate the future, make decisions,
learn from the wrong decisions to make right decisions and pass on
our accumulated knowledge and experience to our children, so that
they are not forced to reinvent the wheel.

Where in all this, then, are feelings? How are they linked to
our capacity for choice and learning? Contrary to much popular
literature which sees feelings as opposite or alternative to rationality, they are the instruments of reasoning. Because we are intelligent creatures—meaning that we are not bound to stilted and
patterned behavior—we are capable of and dependent upon using
choice to decide our futures. Feelings become guides to that choice.
They are a form of fine-tuning, directing the ways in which we will
manipulate our environment. There are remembered and painful
feelings which discourage repetition of the actions that produced
them. There are feelings of mastery, joy and pride which drive us
to new frontiers of creativity. Grief and despair warn us of dangers
that go beyond the physical and threaten the psychological and
emotional realm of existence.

Some situations, however, demand action quickly, before rational analysis can operate. Such emergency emotions fire the rapid-
alerting devices we inherited from our more primitive forebears. In
certain emergency situations the emotions of fear and anger will
initiate physiological actions to protect us before the processes of
reasoning can even figure out that we are in danger. We will intuit,
or smell out, danger. Our body, in its wisdom, prepares us for the
fight or flight before our capacities to analyze the danger can possibly operate. It is an early-warning system which initiates its own
arming devices. Feelings not only signal the behavior to be taken
but initiate the visceral process essential for the adaptive moves.
The adrenaline is pumping and the proper muscles are tensed for
the action before we are conscious of the steps for which they are
preparing us.

Lower forms of animals have behavior responses almost as fixed as the actions of machines. With the emergence of even the limited intelligence one sees in some primitive animals, flexibility and variability emerge. When one approaches the level of human development, instinct is constantly modified by the awareness of variable choices for survival. Intelligence—alone—permits learning by experience. Experience then permits modification of crude instinctual patterns to fit the maze equivalents in everyday life.

Beyond intelligence, *Homo sapiens* has two other extraordinary capacities: imagination—one form of creative thinking; and a capacity to transmit knowledge across generations—a product of symbol formation and the development of language. The interplay between imagination and reason, acting on instinctive emotion, is ingenious and complicated. Any emotion we experience, whether fear, rage, or another, can distort the memory of the events that precipitated it. The emotions can enhance and maintain in memory the terror of a particular event—for example, a near-drowning as a child, so that all exposure to bodies of water can be terrifying. Emotional needs can suppress a memory of pain—as in childbirth —facilitating a new experience in this area.

The capacity for symbol formation permits us to learn from the past and to anticipate the future. We need not wait for the predator to charge us; we need not even wait to see it on the horizon. We can utilize symbols, signs or antecedents of the event as though they were the actual experience. We can learn that one does not walk in certain swamps at certain times. That latter judgment involves complicated abstractions. Once bitten by a snake, we draw conclusions about a category: *snakes.* We then draw conclusions about the dangerousness of *different* snakes, based on size, color and the like. We catalogue whole blocks of information that define snakes and, beyond that, their ecology and habits. And finally, we can write books about snakes, or simply tell stories, to communicate our experience to future generations so that they may learn less painfully and dangerously a lesson in survival. This capacity for generalizing knowledge can turn out to be a mixed blessing. Often what we perceive as a signal of danger may not be a true prediction but simply a distortion introduced by our own specific past and our own sensitivity. If we have experienced something too strongly in the past—an oppressive authority in the figure of a brutal parent— we may anticipate it where we ought not, and perceive it where it does not exist. All authority figures may provoke fear and rage.

Still, anticipation is a powerful instrument. It allows for strength and stability beyond sheer weight, size and animal power. Anticipation and prediction in matters of survival not only help prepare us to meet the assault or run from it but can allow us to modify the situation so that there will be no assault at all. We can build fences and institute preventive measures (quench the fire, dam the stream, support the collapsing tree, mollify the antagonist, propitiate the boss, lie, cajole, seduce). Unlike animals that use anticipation of danger only for fight or flight, we can change the very nature of the reality. We are in that sense coauthor with nature of our future, not merely passive subjects of it. But like the other great adaptive maneuvers, this also leaves us vulnerable to false alarms. What we anticipate may be only products of our oversensitized imagination. The rage we feel may be triggered by an unreal danger, the echo of a similar but not identical situation from the past, and the enemy we attack may be only one of our imagination. We may end up "protecting ourselves" against that which never meant us harm.

And here is the danger. We are capable of actually facilitating that which we dread through defensive maneuvers that were both unnecessary and self-destructive, as does the paranoid person. There is no question that fear still serves its functions. We live in a world of danger, and often we must run from that danger or protect ourselves through more sophisticated versions of flight. The question remains whether in our complicated civilization any of the true dangers that confront us is susceptible to direct physical attack. If not, of what earthly use is the mobilization of the body for such an attack?

If we return now to the ordeal of that seven-minute cab ride and examine the emotions of the participants in that small drama, what purpose was served by all that rage? Whose life was made more secure? Whose safety was enhanced? Whose position was protected? Whose reputation fulfilled? Anger has become endemic in the city and independent of its original purposes. It is the thermostat stuck always at hot. We have made anger obsolescent as an adaptive tool in modern times. Why has this happened? How could a biological tool so central to our ascendance on this earth become so nonutilitarian, so maladaptive in so short a period of time?

The terrible efficiency of cultural as compared with biological forces for changing human nature and behavior is unsettling our adaptive patterns.[5] We have altered the nature of the world we occupy with a speed that is unnatural to the ordinary pace of biological evolution. At the same time we have altered ourselves in ways that a mutation/survival mechanism could have achieved, if at all, only in millions of years. With natural selection, only the useful mutation is likely to survive. Our rapid cultural "mutations" can flourish, at least for the short term, independent of their long-term survival value. What are we, then, to do with this powerful biological device for survival, fixed by millions of years of adaptation and now made obsolescent by a mere few thousand years of culture? That inquiry may be essential for the survival of our species.

The machinery of emotion operates mechanically and autonomously, beyond our control and often our knowledge. Whether the threat is real or only imagined; and even if it is real, whether attack is possible, plausible or even conceivable, the machinery operates on us and within us. It spurs us to actions which may now be maladaptive and in conflict with that which our rational self tells us is in our best interest. It may drive us to self-destructive behaviors. It may force us to ignore crucial survival signals. A runaway emotion is a dangerous thing. We are still threatened, but rarely by anything so simple to respond to as direct assault.

We have constructed a civilization that, for the most part, protects us from the onslaught of other life forms or the uncivilized within our species. We have invented the law to institutionalize our security and our values. We resist even the elements. And still we see ourselves endangered. What threatens this triumphant species, *Homo sapiens,* during a period in which he has fulfilled the Biblical prophecy of his supremacy over the "fowls of the air, and the beasts of the earth, and the fishes of the sea"? What frightens us so? We are out of the jungle and we still do not feel safe.

24

3. What Threatens Us?

Rage and fear are "emergency emotions"[1] established biologically, in those barbaric aeons before civilization, to protect us from danger when the meaning and nature of "danger" were unequivocal. A threat to our survival was present. The danger was real and physical —a beast, an enemy horde, a rebellious kinsman.

Rage sets in motion the machinery for a frontal physical assault: appropriate skeletal muscles are tensed; the autonomic system moves to increase the supply of adrenaline and redistribute the blood flow of the body; certain muscles are contracted and opposing ones relaxed. The animal becomes an armed instrument for physical assault. But assault on what? What dangers remain for civilized man that are satisfactorily resolved by clubbing? Often it is not the enemy we face but his agent; more often than not it is not even a person but a paper. How does one attack a paper? With one's teeth? In addition, because threats these days are so rarely direct and physical, we are less capable of distinguishing between real and fancied threats, and we may be constantly arming ourselves for dangers that exist only in our imagination. We are left with a set of built-in biological mechanisms, directives and signals in the area of anger that diminish rather than enhance our chances for survival.

In modern life danger arrives deviously and elliptically. Since danger is defined in terms of the relative power differential between us and the threat, anything that diminishes us performs the equivalent of enhancing the danger. Anything that is even perceived as weakening us will be interpreted as lessening our capacity to cope and survive. No new element of danger need be introduced into our lives to make us less secure. Simply raise doubts about our strength, reliability or stature, diminish self-respect or self-confidence, and the same environment seems more hazardous. It is this latter pathway that conducts most of the stressful stimuli in modern times. We are most likely to feel threatened when we sense disapproval, deprivation, exploitation and manipulation, frustration, betrayal or humiliation. These are the slings and arrows of modern life. These are the lions and tigers that stalk our civilized environment, and we have sharpened our senses so that we detect their signs everywhere.

Fear and anger were designed to serve as responses to threats to our survival. To our *survival*—not to our pride, status, position, manhood or dignity. Yet somehow we have developed in our minds a crucial linkage between affronts to our status of even a minimal measure and the very sense of our survival. We respond to an affront with biological defenses appropriate for assaults. We experience these affronts as though they were threats to survival.

These are the psychological "assaults" that threaten our security and arouse our anger.

DISAPPROVAL

While biologists were the pioneers in research into stress, even they neglected to adequately appreciate the uniqueness of our species. The human being is *sui generis*. Nowhere is this more evident than in the striking difference between human development and that of other species. And almost every aspect of our peculiar development will influence our future definitions of danger and safety.

Relatively uncomplicated, undifferentiated animals develop in a short gestation period and are born ready to face life alone. Generally speaking, the more complicated the animal, the longer the gestation period. By the time we reach such higher mammals as the elephant, there is a gestation period of twenty-two months. But *Homo sapiens,* the most complicated of animals, has a relatively short gestation period. Beyond that, he will be born, unlike most mammals, in a ridiculously helpless state, and he will remain helpless for a percentage of his life expectancy that is disproportionately large compared with that of his mammalian relatives.

The human infant is capable of neither flight nor fight. He is capable of something related to fear and something related to rage (parents quickly learn to distinguish between furious cries for attention and cries of terror or distress). The infant cannot possibly perceive his survival in terms of avoiding the source of danger. He does not even recognize sources of danger. He is incapable of overcoming even minimal danger with his limited capacities for coping. Survival therefore can never have been originally visualized by the infant in terms of either personal strength, power or any devices that relied on the services of the self. Survival in the early stages is dependent not on ourselves but on others. The first method of survival is neither fight nor flight but something akin to clutch or cling.[2]

It may be a stretch of the imagination to even talk about emotions in the first days of life. It may be more accurate to discuss sensations. Nonetheless, early neonatal development suggests that something akin to true emotions exists. We will never know for sure, since the capacity to communicate is so limited; the essential feeling, or subjective aspect of the emotion, will always be unconfirmable.

Let us assume that this early stage of life is dominated by sensations and perhaps even an undifferentiated sense of self in an environment only dimly realized and perhaps not yet even separated from the self. The emerging consciousness of the baby is intriguing to speculate about. What does he think? He certainly is aware of the discomfort of the cold wet diaper, the pain from the empty stomach, the harshness of the bright light. He responds to the pain or discomfort—probably not voluntarily—with a cry. If the cry is unattended, if the pain or distress is unrelieved, he increases the intensity of the scream. Eventually that scream begins to resemble the rage of a wounded animal. Somewhere along that line of communication a concerned adult will be aroused and attend to the need. A child, unaware of such things as diapers and talc, schedules, diurnal rhythms and sleepless nights, will simply recognize a relief from the distress. It is quite possible—and some researchers have suggested as much—that the infant directly equates the scream with the relief of the pain, as though the scream were directly converted into the food or comfort, without recognizing any intervening agent. If this is so, then he may impute a certain kind of omnipotence to his expressed rage.

This blissful state of magical omnipotence cannot possibly last long. In a very short time the infant begins to differentiate himself from his environment. He notices. He identifies people and things. He separates self from other, person from thing, friend from stranger. Sometime in his first few months the infant begins to face the "facts of life." And the facts are much different from that which may have been his earliest conception. Of course he is not an omnipotent figure. He is a totally helpless creature, incapable of ensuring his own comfort, let along his own survival. Such a precipitous fall from power would unquestionably produce a depression in an adult. Some child psychoanalysts, specifically Melanie Klein,[3] have suggested that this is exactly what happens in the development of an infant. If a depression does develop it will be short-lived, because the infant will soon discover that while he is not omnipotent, there are those about him who seem to be. Food, nurture, comfort, all the necessities of survival are supplied by figures in his environment who have the capacity to ensure his survival. Meeting the needs of survival is then delegated to the parents, and in a caring household security once more prevails.

There is danger, however. What if the parents disappear? What if they are not available, "forget" their responsibilities, stop caring, withdraw their love? From these considerations emerges the great threat of early life: separation—often visualized in terms of abandonment and isolation. The first response to separation is invariably fear, followed quickly by rage. The fear of abandonment is one that survives, often in disguised and complicated forms, well into adulthood, and we will rage at any suggestion of neglect by those whom we love and on whom we depend. This anger is testament to our need for love and our awareness of this dependence.

Sometimes automatically, but often consciously, the parent will begin the process of educating the child toward independence. This may be prompted by a recognition that it is the responsibility of a parent to nurture independence; it may also arise, prematurely, from fatigue, boredom and impatience; or it may emerge naturally from some biologically guided psychological shift in the attitudes of a parent toward the developing child.

A new message will be directed to the child. He will now be expected to conform to certain standards. The process of socialization is beginning. One powerful technique in the training of a child is the granting or withholding of approval. The parent can also use various forms of direct disapproval or punishment. In either case the message is clear: at a time when he is still helpless, still impotent, still incapable of managing his own affairs, the child is being instructed that survival is quite possible through the agency of those around him, but to receive such services it is necessary that those around him love and approve of him. It is not every little boy or girl who gets taken to the zoo by Mommy or Daddy. It is not every little boy or girl who is "lucky" enough to have veggies. To refuse to eat the veggies is an affront to a privileged position. Conform your behavior to that which is expected by the loving parent and you will enhance that love and ensure the benefits of that love.

There has now been a subtle but significant elaboration in the dependency lesson. Not only is survival dependent on other beings, but it is essential that those others be loving. For those others to provide their services, they must value and be concerned about you. Abiding lessons are carried out of those first few years of life: He who is loved is safe. Our power is a vicarious one and is often measured best by the capacity to please the all-powerful figures of the parents. The most dangerous thing in the world is not to be weak—we all manage to survive the ludicrous weakness and inadequacy of our infancy: the most dangerous thing in the world is to be unloved.

Children will begin to test the limits of parental love. Demands will be made, and when met the demands will be extended. Often the parent will be unaware of the fact that what is requested is unimportant, a mere symbol allowing the frightened child to determine the boundaries of that love, always hoping to find an ever-expanding frontier. Eventually the endurance of the most loving parent will be exhausted and anger will emerge. The child will respond with fear and anger in return. In the best of circumstances this battle for limits will eventually force the child into a growing awareness of his own resources and, with luck, the discovery of an independent mode of action.

Luck or no luck—loving, understanding and compassionate though the parents may have been—none of us will enter adult life without that crucial sense of vulnerability which makes us feel threatened when someone of importance withdraws his love from us, or when some other threatens that love.

The greatest rage over loss of love is occasioned when the love is more symbolic than real; when attachments are tentative; when the "love" is a metaphor of worth. In romantic literature, and unfortunately often in courts of law, the fact that one murdered for love is seen as evidence of the intensity of the feeling. The intensity of the attachment is then used to mitigate the guilt or exculpate the act. The facts are usually quite otherwise. It is usually the individual whose attachments are the most symbolic who is driven to the fury of assault and murder when rejected. A truly loving person for whom attachments come easily may feel a profound sense of deprivation and diminution. He may even be grief-stricken by the real loss of that which he valued dearly; but limiting his response will be an awareness of his worthiness of love and an unconscious sense that he will therefore be capable of rediscovering it. This does not necessarily come easily and does little in the immediate period to relieve the grief that is felt over the loss of a loved person.

The rage involved in crimes of passion is often so extraordinary that it is a clue to the nature of the crime. The young person's body found in the woods penetrated with sixty stab wounds is not likely to be the victim of an offended stranger, but that of a "lover," particularly if it is a frustrated, rejected or impotent lover. To lose the only love one feels capable of, to lose the "undeserved" love that one has when one feels unlovable and unentitled to love is to strike at the heart of one's security. Crimes of passion are euphemisms. They are, more accurately, crimes of humiliation.

While few of us will be driven to killing rage, most will be threatened by withdrawal of love, and sustained by its expression. The more dependent the person, the more reassurance he will need. At an extreme of insecurity, any criticism will constitute a threat. It is not necessary for there to be rejection or abandonment or loss of a love object. It is necessary simply for someone to raise questions about lovability or essential worth to produce a sense of stress, inducing either a frightened or an angry response.

If logic prevailed and we were truly independent, temperate people, we would not feel anger when unfairly criticized. We would recognize that the criticism is invalid. In the larger social world beyond the family few feel secure. The instruments of survival are not necessarily within ourselves. Any criticisms can be seen as questioning our power and competence. In addition, in this complicated world, where real power is stripped from the physical sources with which it was originally associated, the perception of others may truly define our potency. In such situations perceived capacity for survival is independent of any correlation with fact or reality. We are only as strong as people think we are. If we are viewed as having power, if we are treated with awe or fear, it is the equivalent of vesting us with that power, since more often than not the ultimate proof of the validity of that power will never be tested.

One of the strangest and most perplexing situations in the development of the child occurs as he approaches late adolescence. On the physical level the power of the parent over the child passes only too quickly. There are very few sixteen-year-old boys who could not, if they chose to, "handle" their fathers and certainly their mothers. Beyond the physical, the child, particularly of the middle class, will maintain a financial dependency on his parents. Even here, in an actual test, he could generally survive on his own. The power of the parent is vested in the *assumptions* of the child, and is best maintained when those assumptions are never put to the test. Both parties in a good relationship avoid the ultimate power struggle that would strip the relationship of its illusions. It serves the purposes of the child as well as those of the adult to perceive the balance of power in a direction different from where it physically rests. In a technological society, the period of dependency must be stretched even beyond the extravagantly prolonged period mandated by biology to allow time for the child to develop the skills and training necessary for functioning as an adult in a complex work world.

Similarly, in less loving relationships than the family, intimidation is often sufficient to allow one individual to control a group. The assumptions that establish a pecking order within a group are often subliminal and unarticulated. Worse, they are often unproved and inaccurate. As a result, an inferior bully may control a group as long as the controlled choose not to test the hypothesis of his power. Ironically, it may take only a moderate and not particularly aggressive outsider to see through the Emperor's clothes.

Given the residual association of love and survival and given the fact that most of us operate in a world of assumptions that are never tested, suggestions of our unlovability or our unworthiness invariably are perceived as a threat and will be answered with fear or anger.

BETRAYAL

Sensitivity to approval and disapproval is always at its most intense in loving situations. It is not surprising that most of us reserve most of our anger for those we love. When we are denied small signals of affection from sources from which we expect only small tokens of affection—for example, casual friends—we feel "slighted," the very word suggesting the minimal response. When we are denied an expected token of love from those we love, we use a stronger word; although the feeling remains relatively slight, we say we are "hurt." The word "hurt" seems peculiar when used relative to incidents involving small damage. The literal meaning of the word carries with it the recognition that real damage can occur when those we love and depend on disappoint us. Feeling hurt involves a gently painful commingling of strains of sadness, anxiety and anger.

When those we depend on for love and support truly betray that trust, we are outraged. It provokes all our fundamental fears. Abandonment by a source of love is central to our earliest definition of death. It persists in the conception of death sustained by most adults. Death is not our nonbeing. How can we visualize nonbeing when the very act of visualizing is an affirmation of being? To most of us death is being "there"—somewhere—but cut off, isolated and abandoned. Betrayal is a stab at the heart.

Betrayal is also a profound signal of worthlessness. The indifference and disdain of the impersonal world of strangers is balanced by the concern of those who love us. When that love is trivialized or denied, the balance is dangerously dislocated. If those who we assume most value us abandon or discard us, what actual worth can we presume to possess?

Betrayal involves the fear of rejection compounded by the humiliation of deceit. Even if the deceit is a self-inflicted wound based on false assumptions, it carries with it the pain and mortification of false expectations. The betrayed person feels unloved, unsure and used. When he sees this as a product of willful calculation suggesting contempt, the erstwhile loved one is exposed as the enemy, and the rage at this enemy will be compounded by the rage with self for having been accomplice to the deception.

Betrayal is capable of generating the most direct and explosive outpouring of anger. When it is compounded by affront to sexuality, the danger is immense. To both genders, sexuality is a measure of worth and power. Men, in our society, are taught to see their sex as a direct measure of their potency. Manhood carries the mantle of power. Women are taught to see their sexual desirability as the instrument for enlisting that power for their survival. To attack a sense of sexual worth is to strike at the core of both male and female security. It is no wonder that such betrayal will lead to the nightmarish brutality which characterizes so many crimes of passion.

DEPRIVATION

Deprivation is closely related to withdrawal of love but has more complicated roots. Deprivation is not a quantitative phenomenon.

One can be surrounded with the riches of the affluent life and feel deprived, and one can have endured great poverty where everything is measured and counted, stored and rationed and still not feel deprived. Deprivation emerges from a sense of what one has in terms of what one thinks others have. It is a relative feeling. It suggests that somehow or other that which is rightly yours has not been given you—or, worse, has been taken from you. What is rightly yours is usually measured in terms of that which others receive.

Equity and fairness are fundamental needs for peace of mind. The first great outrages of childhood usually involve feeling that somehow or other something has been done, usually by the parent, that was not fair—generally meaning that a sibling "got away with something"; was given something more or better; was allowed a privilege or an indulgence which we were denied.

The Old Testament is probably the richest reservoir of human psychology available. It is not just chance that it abounds in discussion of sibling rivalry; Cain and Abel, Jacob and Esau, Joseph and his brothers. Psychoanalysis, surprisingly, originally cast all rivalry in terms of that great triumvirate, mother, father and child.[4] Its view of rivalry is a very special and limited case. Rivalry in the Oedipal situation is one in which the child never wins. The boy, in competing with his father for the love of his mother, must eliminate the father. But to destroy the father is terrifying to the child, who recognizes his own impotence and understands that his survival depends on the goodwill, the resources and the strengths of that parent. It is even more difficult for a girl, for in competing for her father she must displace that ultimate symbol of nurture in childhood, the mother. To lose the competition with the parent is to reaffirm your helpless state as a child. To win the competition is even more dreadful, for firmly fixed in one's unconscious self-image is the awareness of one's limited resources and one's dependence on the parental figure. To have destroyed that parental figure is a hollow victory indeed, for it is shattering the very vessel that keeps one afloat.

There is a rivalry in childhood that can be won. The average child operates under the assumption that life is a zero-sum game.

He sees a limited amount of time and assumes a limited amount of love and affection. The more a sibling gets, the less is available for him. This competitive aspect may serve useful purposes. It may drive the individual to assertive behavior, to perfection of skills, to creativity and high performance. That it has destructive aspects is only too evident in a competitive society gone haywire. The frightening aspect is in the recognition that this is a competition that can be won. If one destroys the sibling, one gets exclusive possession of the parents. It is one reason that the death of a sibling, particularly during one's adolescence, is so devastating a blow. Since the sibling has so often been "wished" dead, and since to the unconscious wishing *can* make it so, the burden of guilt can be immense and carried through a lifetime.

The fact that sibling rivalry can be won carries with it the equally ominous suggestion that it can be lost. No wonder children examine and measure the relative gifts of affection from parents with instruments of the finest calibration. What they are measuring is not just affection but survival.

In a society as individualistic as our own, some means for dissipating and controlling feelings of competition are essential. Play is one such device. It is a cliché that one understands more about the personality of a colleague in an hour on a tennis court than in a week of business meetings or general living-room socializing. The competitive aspects are real, and yet the results, at least in terms of survival, are minimal. Sports allow us to act out our fantasies of conquest with little risk of actual pain or destruction. This is particularly true when our competitive activities involve only watching *others* play. Spectator sports allow us to identify with supermen, to risk humiliation to gain victory, with little damage if any to our real position in life. The fact that betting has become so much a factor in spectator sports may represent a need to inject some risk of real pain to enhance the jaded appetite of vicarious competition.

In games the competition may be playful, but the agony is real and the anger is there. The rage that can arise in a mixed-doubles tennis game where husbands and wives—which is to say loved ones —are playing together is almost palpable. Here the competition may be compounded by the inadequate "support" of one's ally (spouse). Court manners and courtliness can control the discharge. It is unlikely that one will see a husband beaten to death by his wife on the tennis court, but if wishes could kill, courts would be as strewn with bodies as the jousting fields of the Middle Ages.

Competition on the job is a much different matter. Real reward and punishment are at stake here. This need not involve risk at the level of hunger or loss of the wherewithal for clothing or shelter. The rewards of affluence have a real value, but while expensive goods are usually better than inexpensive ones, this represents no more than a small percentage of our joy in them; they tend to give greater pleasure through their advertisement of status and power. The replication of family dynamics in the office place has been a badly underestimated factor in success or failure in business. A boss's approval may presage a promotion or a raise, and therefore is valued as a signal of future reward. Close examination of the dynamics in a business community reveals that what passes for the means is often the true end. The raise or the promotion is valued because it is a sign of the boss's approval. The approval is often the driving force and ultimate need. Time spent alone in the company of a charismatic leader of a corporation is like a stolen moment on the lap of a mother. It is cherished and delighted in not just for its ultimate implications, but for its own sake. Beyond time, other symbols of pleasure or love or approval are almost as welcome. The larger office, the corner space, the extra window are the Teddy bears and tricycles of adult office life.

A strange reversal has occurred. The symbolic event has become more important than the real event it was designed to represent. This is a crucial, little-understood element of modern social life which creates more distress and social havoc than has been imagined. An authority is perceived as having the equivalent of life-and-death control over his subordinates. Signs of his approval become as critical for security as the signs of parental approval once were. These factors hold true even when no real threat to physical survival is involved. It does not matter that the worker is well beyond the poverty level, that what is at risk is no longer food and shelter but only material accretions. After the authority has been established and a position of dependency ingrained, the dynamic has a life of its own. The need for approval, acting on the vulnerable child that exists within the adult, becomes paramount. Approval no longer need serve survival; it becomes a desired end in itself. Status indicators become more important than actual wealth. At that point all that remains for us to do with the wealth that we accumulate is translate it into different status symbols. We trade in the Ford for the Jaguar, rationalizing that we are getting superior transportation while attempting to ignore the expense and unreliability of that fragile automobile.

The symbolic overlay is what makes us so sensitive to questions of fairness and equity. If our best is not acknowledged as that of others seems to be, if our labor goes unrewarded, if we feel deprived of our just deserts, the anger and resentment generated will first contaminate our relationship with those who are depriving us and later be extended, illogically, to those who are given more than we are in the same situation. We may start by recognizing that they are simply the fortunate recipients of a largesse that accidentally came to them instead of us. We will hold this view for only a limited time. Eventually the resentment toward the authority figure must be displaced. We cannot afford to sustain anger for too long toward those in power. We will try to dissipate it by deflecting it. The logical deflection is to our colleague, co-worker, sibling, neighbor—whoever seems to be awarded *our* share of the prize.

Feeling deprived is akin to feeling cheated. A chronic state of deprivation can lead to the smoldering anger of political resentment. Deprivation will always be measured in relative terms by comparison of that which we are getting for our efforts with what our neighbor is getting—not by some equivalence with a less affluent culture. Political deprivation operates under the same rules as personal. The source of the deprivation will eventually be forgotten, and he who has—anyone who has—will be the enemy.

With continued feeling of inequity we may expand the personally experienced deprivation into a broader view that will encompass all society. It is not just one authority, but all authority that is at fault. When the deprivation can be associated with station, gender, race or class, the social order will be viewed as the unfair agent and unfairness will be relabeled injustice. Alienation is almost always a product of the resentment that comes from living in a society perceived as unjust. Acts against the social order are viewed differently when the social order is seen as supporting an immoral state of affairs. The unjust society is an evil society, which commands neither our allegiance nor our respect.

Injustice focused purely on ourselves can lead to a paranoid adjustment. If extended to our group it can lead to an alienated or revolutionary disposition (the latter can also accommodate paranoia). The presence of a paranoid element does not invalidate or exculpate the actual inequity or injustice; truth is neither verification nor refutation of paranoid assumptions.

Obviously there is a strong relationship between the withdrawal of love and the feeling of deprivation. Both of them build on the dependency adaptation with which we all inevitably must start life. Given the biological fact of the dependent, helpless state of the human infant, there is no way to eradicate from his experience the dependency adaptation. These early lessons are well learned and never forgotten. The dependency adaptation is with us and will always be there. Methods of controlling the resentment that stems from inequity will have to attack the inequity, and particularly the tension-producing sources of inequity.

One source of inequity is not readily available for resolution. When a child is severely deprived of love, attention and care, no amount of later restitution may be sufficient compensation. The child raised in true deprivation as a product of illegitimacy, broken home or alcoholic or otherwise abusive parents may be so scarred as to preclude any repair. He may carry his angered sense of personal injury through experiences of affluence and good fortune. He will feel cheated in the presence of abundance, and his anger and resentment will convert true privilege into perceived deprivation. We may be forced to accept the painful recognition that there exists an unredeemable group. For others there remains hope.

Whenever an individual finds himself in a position of dependency, he will recast the current reality in terms of the helpless phase of his childhood, evoking all the urgency and volatility of that earlier state. We thus run the risk that he will magnify the danger in his situation and act accordingly. Since we cannot extricate the memories of the early dependency experience, we must reduce the population of those who are forced to feel dependent.

In the past [5] I have drawn the distinction between exogenous and endogenous dependency. These somewhat awkward terms are meant to distinguish those forms of dependency which are imposed from the outside from those which are inherent in the individual. Endogenous dependents would include the infant, the senile, the severely ill and the retarded. The exogenously dependent would be the unemployed, the student, the aged whom inflation has deprived of their autonomy and other impoverished groups. Means must be found to support the pride as well as the needs of these latter populations. Beyond simple decency, cultural survival will demand it.

EXPLOITATION AND MANIPULATION

The three mechanisms described above—disapproval, betrayal and deprivation—exploit our inner feelings of dependency; unsure of our own capacities, we feel our survival threatened when the value and esteem in which we are held by the powerful authority figures or their representatives come into question. There are, however, direct assaults on our self-worth, direct affronts to pride and confidence. Exploitation and manipulation deprive us of the special status inherent in being a human being. When we feel used the fusion between fear and anger is broken and we are likely to feel pure anger.

It is ironic that two words so close in root and derivation as being "used" and being "useful" should have almost antithetic meanings. To feel useful is to be enhanced. To be useful to someone else's needs is a tribute to some resource within us which can benefit that other. Our usefulness is an index of our worth. We have something of value, something that is capable of giving pleasure, comfort or strength to another. Feeling useful is a restorative emotion. To be used, however, has exactly the opposite implication. To feel used is to feel that we are not a person but a vehicle. It involves the separation of our services from ourselves. Instead of a partner and ally, we have become a conduit, an instrument for the satisfaction of the other person's needs. We have been diminished; dehumanized; reduced from a person to a thing.

The difference may be as simple as whether the announced purposes of the use were agreed on in advance; whether we were party to the bargain. The very thing that when freely given produces pride, when taken surreptitiously is perceived as humiliation.

Obviously, whenever lying and deceit are involved a sense of being used emerges. Even when it is done with no malice, being lied to can make us feel manipulated. This "handling" of our "self" by another diminishes us by equating that self with a thing. We go through life exposed to continual ambiguous situations in which we cannot be sure whether the give-and-take is part of a shared amiability or whether we are being used. When lying and deceit are involved, we sense, often unaware, that a great "moral imperative" has been violated. We know that we have been manipulated, used as a means to someone else's end.

In another context I once described multiple uses of the word "put" in relation to people. The "put-down," the "put-on," being "put upon." The use of the word "put" is informative. It is a verb particularly associated with objects, and we are made to feel like an object in all these contexts. The put-down directly advertises the other person's superiority to us; but in a sense, the put-on is worse. Here we are led down the garden path to humiliation by our very trust in the individual. Everyone resents being conned.

Whenever we feel used as a thing we feel uncomfortable, and that explains our anger in the face of even well-intended manipulation. Whenever we feel we have been controlled or influenced by means that bypass our rationality, our will and our sense of volition, our autonomy has been diminished, and that explains our great anger at being placed in a general category, being pigeonholed. The use of computers in our modern culture is resisted and resented because they assault our image of uniqueness and specialness. A person should be too complex for categorization. Our individuality and our autonomy are structures that support the sense of human dignity.

We are wary of any technological means of changing human

behavior even when they lead to improvements. Things should not be capable of modifying people; people change things. If a pill were invented for improving learning rates it would be viewed with distrust and alarm. The use of drugs by athletes is handled by a massive denial. "Artificial" changes of behavior are accepted only where developed within the context of a medicine.

The medical model presumes a standard of behavior that is normal and, somehow, natural. For example, if there is a "sickness" which causes a natural deficiency in our intelligence we will accept a "cure." Therefore, we would tolerate a drug that would bring us up to our normal potential. This concept of replacement is so standard in medicine that it is unthreatening. The doctors are simply restoring us to a state of normality, which is equated with health, which is equated with goodness, which is equated with the natural order of things. If a pedagogue were to offer a drug to enhance learning and improve concentration, he would be resisted most vigorously. If such a drug were developed, the only way we could accept it would be if we first invented a disease for which we could call this a treatment. Once a disease was discovered that was characterized by poor attention span and impaired learning capacity, the drug could be dispensed by a doctor. Placing it under the medical model removes the stigma and implies replacement (normalizing) rather than improvement (tampering).

We do not see ourselves as being manipulated by physicians. They are restoring us to health. We would be likely to see ourselves as being manipulated by educators, even if the purpose were simply to make us superior people. There is suspicion of that kind of superiority. It seems unnatural. These arguments are not susceptible to logic, the distinctions between natural and unnatural in human behavior being at best inexact. Nonetheless, they are ingrained in basic biases.

Even when the purposes of the "manipulation" are unselfishly intended to satisfy a common or personal good, we are suspicious. High technology works too efficiently; it changes behavior in a way that makes us a passive partner in the action. In all other areas we are inclined to take the most economical and fastest road. In terms of changing human behavior the very technological efficiency frightens us because we are then seen as the products of our own machinery. We will prefer the slower but manageable methods of education in which we are an active involved agent. Perhaps we are right to do so. But we do pay a price.

Many people live in such fear of being used that they will close themselves off from relationships of potential worth so as not to risk pain, anger and humiliation. They will protect themselves at unreasonable cost. It is certainly not the worst thing to be used occasionally, even in the worst sense. Far more damaging is to deteriorate into that quasi-paranoid state in which every approach is viewed with cynicism, every request seen as exploitation. Where wariness and suspicion reign, trust and joy in people are abandoned. To go through life in an armored car is to be safe—and alone.

FRUSTRATION

Anything that makes us feel less whole, less powerful, less useful and less valued brings us into a sense of danger. We depend on others and the respect of others to support our self-esteem. But it is not just in our relationship with others that we can be made to feel inadequate. Our self-confidence is equally founded on ourselves and our own performance. When respect for the latter begins to erode, survival is threatened. Modern researchers have placed great emphasis on the relationship between frustration and anger.[6] Many original theories tended to have a hydraulic view of the relationship between frustration and rage. The drives and impulses for work and mastery were seen as building in intensity. When these drives were thwarted, a backward tension built up, like that of dammed water, which could be converted into the emotion of anger. Anyone exposed to frustration in attempting even a minor task is aware of how quickly the irritability level can be raised and anger produced.

Each person has his own paradigm of the agonies of minor frustration. My frustration tolerance is particularly low in dealing with small parts and fine works—the tiny screw that must be positioned into the small opening under the extended ridge that is protected by a delicate filament to which is attached a wire that must not be disturbed. It is a situation that even in anticipation is sufficient to get my hands trembling with anticipated rage and frustration, and the trembling in turn is sure to disturb the wire that must remain inviolate for the mechanism to survive. It is the wise person who knows his own poisons and avoids them.

When I am involved with these specific projects, they are rarely related to anything central to my basic survival. It is more likely assembling a toy for a grandchild or attempting a minor repair on a piece of electronic equipment. Why are these frustrations so particularly infuriating? Do these things operate on a hydraulic mechanism? Even if I had a ravenous appetite for music at a moment when a small short occurred in my record player, I doubt that it would be my repressed hunger for music that was great enough to produce such anger. The frustration has nothing to do with my desire to hear music, or any deprivation in this area. It is my own personal ineptitude that threatens and, therefore, angers me. What is disturbing me is my knowledge that *others* can handle these matters quite well and that I seem to be particularly inept. The feeling of being all thumbs is not far from the feeling of having no hands. What enrages me, because it frightens me, is an emerging awareness of inadequacy. Most of us are not frustrated by our inability to climb Mount Everest, make a million or golf like Nicklaus. It is changing the washer, balancing the checkbook, tying the knot with the short ends that undoes us. The apparent easiness of the task suggests that others can do it, and often they can. Our failure is more dramatic for being so relative. If I am incapable even here, where others succeed, what does that say about the worth and reliability of my self?

We can guard against a sense of impotence by deflecting the anger from the self to others; by concentrating on what created the problem rather than who could not resolve it. It is here that children and spouses become particularly convenient. To return to the example of the record player: if one can assume that the damage to the instrument could conceivably have been done by a child or a spouse, one could divert the stream of anger from oneself, withdraw the attention from one's own inadequacy and find a convenient, culpable target.

A more rational, and less destructive, device for handling the rage of frustration is to make a game of it. If we generate frustration in a nonvital setting, where the true stakes are small—play, not work—we can deflect and defuse it. It can be experienced without any sense of danger, and frustration can be almost pleasurable. We generate frustration in games and hobbies. The game of golf is ideal. It is guaranteed to generate such rage. In a certain sense, golf is a noncompetitive game. When adults play golf together there are two games going on simultaneously. There is the competition with the others, as in tennis. This is relatively unimportant, even when betting is involved. Then there is the competition against a defined and quantified statement of perfection. In tennis the opponents' ineptitude can be interpreted as your skill. Not in golf. Here there is an absolute measurement against par. For the most part, golfers in a foursome are involved in something akin to the parallel play of children. They cover the same ground in the same time span, but the real game is a solitary one. It is a competition between what one can do on a specific day and what one likes to think of as one's normal game. It is the fury with the imperfect self that so annoys us. This is neither a paradox nor a contradiction. The appeal of this activity, beyond simply the safe direction of frustration, is in the search for perfectibility. We enjoy hobbies because they test us to our limits. We enjoy games because they stretch us, and the occasional perfectly executed chip shot or passing backhand excites us with the promise of what we are capable of doing when everything works. In addition, if one prevails over frustration it leads to a sense of triumph. It has the same result, I assume, as reaching the summit of the mountain. It is precisely because of the frustration, precisely because of the difficulty, precisely because of the failures and pain endured that the achievement is valued.

These small frustrations and the angers they produce are in many ways similar to low levels of anxiety. There is a pleasurable involvement with these emotions. The anxiety that precedes a non-vital competition, or an amateur performance of any sort, has in it an element of lift. There is the awareness that no real danger is involved, particularly when we are reasonably confident of our level of performance. In addition, anger and anxiety at a low level add excitement and self-awareness. Any enhancement of the self as a performer and doer contains within it elements of pleasure.

Of an entirely different nature and intensity is the general frustration of day-to-day existence. Here there is no element of play; nor is there necessarily an expectation of ultimate achievement. Chronic frustration drains self-confidence and diminishes self-esteem. We no longer see ourselves as successful doers. We no longer respect ourselves as reliable instruments of our own pleasure and our own security. The frustration of menial, unrewarding, unchallenging work that has no beginning or end, no product or pride; that leads nowhere, with no hope of surcease, is a pleasureless and dehumanizing experience. It damages our respect for ourselves as instruments of our own pleasure. It does, however, still leave essentially intact our sense of honor and worth. The Protestant work ethic, by valuing performance above pleasure, protects our self-respect. As a worker we are fulfilling our responsibility and duty.

If the value of our work is brought into question or treated with contempt, or if we are deprived of our capacity to work, that is a different order of things. With unemployment we are frustrated in our ability to fulfill our image as a worker. When such frustration is imposed from outside, the resulting diminution of self-pride and self-respect is seen as the product of an assault. Someone has invaded the repository of our dignity and robbed us of the instruments of self-respect.

Frustration will always be most malignant when it involves those aspects central to the purpose of life. Invariably they fall into the areas defined by Freud as *Liebe und Arbeit*—love and work. Most of us are not driven to the extreme rage that leads to murder or suicide because the frustrations we experience do not generally test us to our limits. When such events do occur, the anger is immense, evil and ugly. Violent cases of frustrated rage are of particular interest because, through hyperbole, they indicate to us the feelings most of us control, deny, displace or act out minimally. The passion in crimes of passion is the rage of frustrated potency, not of frustrated love. Violent crimes of passion are the product not of rejected lovers but of impotent lovers. In one typical case that I studied, a teenage boy stabbed to death a prepubescent girl in what was described as a sexual crime. It would have been better described as an asexual crime. This inhibited young man had never been able to achieve an orgasm. One Christmas, while working in a department store, he lured a child who had come to visit Santa Claus to the stockroom where he worked. He had the eight-year-old girl undress, and he attempted to masturbate while looking at her nude body. After twenty minutes of frustrating inability to reach an ejaculation, he began to rage. The frightened child started to cry, and in a combination of rage and terror he picked up a knife and stabbed her repeatedly to death.[7]

The psychoanalytic term to cover threats to potency and power is castration anxiety—a strange term, to say the least. The word "anxiety" implies a minimal amount of terror. The emotion is practically never simply anxiety but terror commingled with rage. It is also a term that unmistakably reflects a male-dominated society, a society which viewed being "a man" as the equivalent of being strong and powerful. Loss of potency or power was visualized in terms of the loss of male genitalia. The term has now come to be used for both men and women and to symbolize all those feelings of powerlessness which derive from our loss of confidence in ourselves as securers of our futures.

VIOLENCE

Withdrawal of love, deprivation, diminution, exploitation and frustration are the beasts of the modern-day jungle. We are more often threatened by these attacks than by actual violence. Yet actual violence does play a part in our life. And while most city dwellers have never been mugged, the amount of conversation about mugging that goes on between adults at dinner parties, between parents and children and among children in their schoolyard play is testament to how important a factor it is in the psyche of the city. The actual world we live in—except in cases of extremis (hunger, cold, unemployment and other privations)—is less important than the world as we perceive it. The slights, the attacks, the disgraces, the frustrations are equally painful whether real or imagined.

46

Most of us endure our frustrations and humiliations without resort to animal attack. We accept the deprivation without attempting to rectify it by physically attacking either the agent of our deprivation or the fortuitously privileged. The fact that others do not behave in this way is particularly outraging. We are infuriated because we are aware of precisely the same impulses within ourselves which we do not indulge. If we can feel as they feel and not act as they act, their lack of restraint is a double offense against our deprivation.

Further, the antisocial behavior of those who indulge their rage is both a threat against and a constriction on our own lives. We must now add fear of violence to the other indignities of modern life. At this point every middle-class person in a large city personally knows someone who has been attacked on the streets. The potential for violence exists everywhere, at all times. No home remains safe, no street secure. Fear is at the ready. Fear and rage are inextricably linked, so that the face of one almost always bears on its obverse the image of the other. We are in a rage—those of us who occupy and must use the city streets—with the violence in the streets, because we are aware of our own "right" to feel violent (we all feel deprived), which our self-discipline keeps us from acting out. We are also in a rage because others do—tempting us to retaliate in kind. And we are in a rage because we are, ultimately, intimidated by that violence. We will join our rage at a society that is less than just and nourishing with our rage at those who frighten us. It is a dangerous amalgam which can lead to a paranoid orientation and the diminution of compassion which is the raw material of bigotry.

HUMILIATION

All the psychological conditions that confront us with a sense of danger are compounded when the emotions we are experiencing are made public. Humiliation is the ultimate degradation. When the "fact" that we are less than lovable is exposed to the public eye, that we are less than potent is announced in the public space, that

47

we are deprived and inadequate becomes part of the public knowledge, we experience humiliation of the most painful order. To our reduced state is added the knowledge that those around us know. This exposure invites potential exploitation—there will always be those who will see in our weakness an opportunity for enhancing their strength. But beyond that, and probably more important, is the shame that accompanies humiliation. We define ourselves, after all, not just as individuals but as members of groups. We take our pride not just in our survival and in our accomplishments but in the acknowledgment of those accomplishments by the group, in the appreciation of our worth by the community. To be reduced as an individual in our own eyes is bad enough. To be shamed before the group compounds our pain in a way that can convert anger into outrage, hurt into humiliation, and ultimately pierce the threshold of our constraint.

It may well be that at some distant time that uncivilized but intelligent beast who was our ancestor realized that he could anticipate physical assault from the demeaning and diminishing behavior that preceded it. An advantage was gained if the rage mechanism that mobilized him was initiated during the early, nonphysical phase of the confrontation. But now the nonphysical *is* the attack. The anger serves no useful purpose and in itself poses an additional risk. Anger is now a renegade emotion which threatens the survival of the species it was "designed" to defend. In order to understand how we might control the generation and expression of anger in our culture we must understand something of its mechanisms—its biology and psychology.

4. The Mechanisms of Anger

Freud once said, "I know of nothing less important for the comprehension of anxiety than the knowledge of the nerve paths by which the excitations travel." [1] While it is true that current physiological theories of emotions have brought us no closer than Freud to understanding them, we are now probably at the threshold of a new era in which a greater understanding may be achieved.

Much of the original research on anger mistakenly regarded this emotion as purely a component of aggression, equating the emotion with action which may or may not be a product of that emotion. This is an inevitable distortion resulting from research that is primarily conducted on lower animals. (Biological research on human anger is pathetically limited.) Only overt behavior could be measured. Feelings, so important an element in human emotions, are not readily examinable in species that do not have the capacity to experience the wide range of feelings available to people or to communicate those feelings they can experience. It is apparent that anger in human beings need not be linked to aggression.

Other complications ensued. Various researchers used different definitions of anger, which helps explain why some theorists evaluated anger as constructive while others saw it as purely destructive. Many of the conflicting research conclusions were predetermined by the specific definition of anger that had motivated the studies in the first place. It is the "Seek and ye shall find" principle which afflicts so much of social-science research.

While very little primary research is yet being conducted on human anger *per se,* there is certainly a greater tendency to focus upon it than there was some fifteen years ago. The fields of psychiatry, physiology and clinical medicine had traditionally viewed the emotion of anger as a rather uninteresting derivative of aggression and hostility. Today it is recognized as a crucial, complex psychophysical phenomenon with wide-ranging implications for mental, physical and social well-being. Medical researchers now pay more attention to anger as an element in healing disease; clinicians now differentiate anger from the rest of the complex of aggression, finding it a key factor in illnesses as diverse as acne, acute depression and rheumatoid arthritis; and physiologists have discovered that aggression is not a unitary biological concept but a mixed bag, an end point with differing and complicated roots. It is the emotion of anger, not the behavior, that may have discrete pathways and specific endocrine mechanisms.

Any emotion is a complex phenomenon with at least three separate elements: one autonomic;[2] one a function of the central nervous system;[3] and one cognitive.[4] With the first two, anger is part of an emotional line that carries us back to our common heritage with lower animals. Any pet owner can recognize the signs of fear and anger in his cat or dog. We are all familiar with the bristling, snarling, exposed-teeth, growling, crouching, lunging gestures of one male dog toward a strange male dog who dares, uninvited, to enter his turf.

This canine behavior is essentially unplanned and uncontrolled. It is prepatterned, with remarkable invariability. The automatic nature of the response can be best appreciated through amusing misperceptions. To an unsophisticated animal, particularly a puppy, any stimulus that is strange and of a certain size can initiate the emergency responses. A puppy will approach a child's large toy, an anchor on the beach, any unfamiliar object of a limited size and conformation with the same menacing behavior that an adult dog would manifest at the approach of his "enemy."

Anger can be modified by fear, its allied emotion in stress, and the interplay between these two emotions is remarkable. They have been referred to in the past as "emergency emotions." Nowadays we are more likely to describe them in terms of stress reaction. Either terminology indicates the activation of physical resources which are intended to serve the animal in facing a specific task requiring heightened concentration, physical strength and maximal stamina. The show of anger also serves an important communicative function. It is a visual display intending to warn, intimidate or challenge the threatening other.

To the evolutionary biologist, the adaptive functions and mal-adaptive hazards of anger have been described in this way: "The angry organism is making an appraisal of his current situation, which indicates that his immediate or long-run survival needs are jeopardized; his basic interests are threatened. Moreover, his appraisal indicates that another organism (or group) is responsible for this threat. Although there are many ways he can go from this appraisal, the tendency is to prepare for vigorous action to correct the situation, quite likely action directed against the person seen as causing or at least manifesting the jeopardy to his needs. The signals are likely to be transmitted to these individuals as well as the organism's own decision-making apparatus. The significant others are then likely to respond in a way that will ameliorate the situation."[5]

The quotation ends with a reassuring optimism. Group animals establish a pecking order, which avoids constant confrontation; once established, the order is a civilizing mechanism to facilitate group cohesion and survival. This nice biological mechanism for stability has not, unfortunately, been retained upward in human adaptation. Or if it is still an inherent part of our genetic endowment, we have modified it through our culture. The "significant other" too often assesses that his basic interests are also at stake in the situation, and whatever "pecking order" exists is often viewed as mutable and questionable. With human beings we are usually ready to enter the power struggle, to test, challenge or confront the order. We have prepared the ground for a violent or aggressive resolution to the problem. In human groups, we have diminished the biological imperative to get along.

In lower animals the rules are always simpler. Aggression is limited, for the most part, to matters involving food, water, sexual objects and the territory that commands these three. In human beings "basic interests" are often elaborate, metaphoric and symbolic, involving such nonbiological factors as status, position, self-esteem, pride, "face" and dignity. Slights to esteem can be measured with the most delicate of balances and injuries viewed with the most magnifying of lenses. The cunning human animal respects the symbol often above the fact. He appreciates the strength and force of money, the relative power of weapons, the importance of allies and allegiances. And he can check and delay response, deceive, anticipate, store grievances. He understands the coming of the seasons.

Nonetheless, our increased understanding of emotions continues to support the fact that, in human beings as in the lower animals, anger is essentially a basic emotional response to stress which alerts, motivates and invigorates the organism to defend its basic interests. Comments Ernest Becker about human anger: "These aggressions . . . represent a reaction to feeling cheated, duped, stripped naked, undermined. The person . . . reacts to assert himself, to show and feel that he is someone to reckon with. Anger generally has this function for the person, as a way of setting things in balance once again."[6]

Already we see that human anger, *per se,* is not invariably a pathologic phenomenon, nor is it always translated into aggressive behavior. By warning the adversary, it may be a form of communication that actually forestalls more violently aggressive arousal and behavior.

What do we know at this point about the "biology" of anger? Where are we in understanding the central (brain) mechanisms and the automatic response (constricted pupils, tensed muscles and the like) of anger? Not too far along, I am afraid. We have not yet adequately charted the anatomy—the structure—of the brain, let alone its physiology or function. Pathways of the brain have remained a mystery even though human anatomists have been producing exquisitely detailed and accurate charts of the musculoskeletal system, for example, for hundreds of years. We do not even know whether all brain function operates through specific pathways.

With the physiology of the brain, like the physiology of the other systems, understanding had to await more profound and basic development in chemistry, physics and biology. This did not occur until the glorious scientific revolution at the end of the nineteenth century. With this new knowledge we moved rapidly ahead in our understanding of the chemistry of the endocrine, musculoskeletal and other systems of the human body. The central nervous system remained an enigma. Only in the last twenty-five years have we seen the stubborn yielding of any significant information in this area.

While our actual understanding may have been enhanced only meagerly, the search for understanding was extensive. The bibliography of the physiology of the central nervous system is massive and cannot adequately be reviewed here. For our purposes a meager outline will have to suffice.

With the pioneering work of Walter Rudolf Hess and his associates[7] in the 1920s the anatomical attempts to understand anger were given their first great breakthrough. These researchers introduced electrodes into various areas of the midbrain, focusing on the thalamus, a nuclear group that was poorly understood but was generally assumed to have some relationship to basic animal drives. When a cat is stimulated by electrodes placed in the thalamus, a specific response occurs. This response proved to be a constant and predictable one. The stimulated cat responded with a defensive posture, arching its back and lashing its tail, in the traditional manner of cats preparing for a fight. This work by Hess was easily replicable by other researchers and caused major excitement in the hope that somehow or other it would lead to an understanding of anger in humans.

Subsequent to this, J. W. Papez[8] began a different line of research, later elegantly extended by others.[9,10] He enlarged the specific focus of the emergency emotions beyond the thalamus into other subcortical structures which also proved to be involved with primitive mechanisms of arousal, metabolism and emotional behavior in general.

This extensive, integrating and coordinating circuit for crude emotional response has come to be called the limbic system. This system is now viewed as the central pathway linking perception on one hand with metabolism and raw emotion on the other. This system includes such readily forgettable areas of brain anatomy as the septal area of the cortex, the corticocingulate and endorhinal areas, the hippocampus and most of the amygdaloidal nuclei. They describe extensive anatomically separated but linked systems stretching throughout the structure of the brain. Much of the research that followed focused on the varying areas of the limbic system. Scientific advances in this area have been steady, but each advance in the laboratory has led to wishful thinking—out loud and in public—about the "promises" such research holds for alleviating the psychological and sociological consequences of anger.

With the advent of psychosurgery,[11] auxiliary information began to emerge from direct experience with human beings. Certain patients with forms of epilepsy intractable to drugs required brain operations for their survival. In the same period lobotomy and cortical ablations were being used as a last-resort treatment for unmanageable psychotics. From both of these sets of studies it appeared that some of the same structures of the limbic system were indeed involved in emotional experience in human beings. Now the generalizations became frenetic.

While this material was promising, caution should have prevailed. Evidence from a number of experiments with animals indicated that the rage which accompanies an animal's aggression was a much different thing from the complex emotion called rage in human beings. Even by the early 1970s physiologists had become increasingly aware that human aggression was much more complex than anything perceived in animals, and that it was "not a unitary phenomenon. There are several kinds of aggressions, each of which has a particular neural and endocrine basis."[12] Further, it was found that a number of experimental psychological and sociological conditions could increase the probability or ferocity of anger. The most effective included frustration, an increase of sexual arousal, hunger and fatigue; others included isolation, overcrowding and sudden disruption of a steady metabolic state such as sleep or meditation.[13] We are back in the streets of the city.

Despite these increasingly complicated differentiations, sweeping generalizations were made about controlling social anger based on limited anatomic studies of specific rage.[14] This was to severely set back this much-needed research on human aggression.[15]

If we know little of the anatomy of human anger and aggression, we know less of its chemistry. Elucidating the neurochemistry of aggression is difficult. Different structures in the brain may produce a variety of different metabolic responses, depending on what chemical is experimentally manipulated and in which part of which structure. How are we to know, at this point, how many of the variables we have controlled? The chemicals themselves may react differently in different locations. And finally, experiments are always conducted with artificially and experimentally induced aggression, inevitably so vastly different from the complicated mechanism in which anger appears in normal life situations.

Two recent research discoveries—one involving drugs found to have specific actions in controlling depression, and the other the discovery of receptors that seem to mediate pleasure through naturally produced chemicals (endorphins) which affect the brain in a similar manner to opiates—give hope that we are finally entering a new era of understanding. But nothing—let me repeat, nothing—can be definitively said at this point about the chemistry of emotion, despite all the claims and counterclaims. For example, many studies have tried to show that levels of a drug called serotonin could be correlated with frequencies of mental hospitalization for psychiatric patients, seasonal patterns of suicide, cyclic fluctuations in the suicide rate, aggravated assaults and psychiatric emergencies.[16] In all these experiments, equally competent researchers have found contradictory results. The evidence is just as confusing in dealing with other neurochemicals such as epinephrine, acetylcholine and dopamine.

That these drugs *in some way* are involved in the regulatory function of emotions seems, at this point, unquestioned; but in *what* way, no one can say—and those who say should not be trusted. Evidence that exists is contradictory or at least open to alternative interpretation.

A more basic argument remains unsettled. Some theorists—from William James down—have predicted that emotions could and would be distinguished from each other physiologically. Other theorists in the tradition of Walter Cannon steadily maintain that emotional differences are colored centrally and that there is no difference between fear and anger, for example, on a physiological level. The advocates of specificity are neither less nor more impressive in their credentials and their determination than those against specificity.[17]

And so, after all this, the biological models are only a hope of the future—assuming that the rampant changes in our sociology, economics and politics allow us an extended future. They offer us little practical use today. While chemistry or surgery may ultimately supply a more elegant and definitive solution in some technological future, we must try to survive until then by utilizing what crude tools are now at hand. We must examine how psychosocial factors may be manipulated to control or channel anger.

It is easy enough to reduce the capacity for anger in lower animals. Even those which seem closely allied to us are programmed by and servants of their own biology. Not so with human beings. We are less efficient than lower animals, but infinitely more adaptable. Because of our cerebral cortex with its capacity for analytic reasoning, we are capable of finding multiple solutions to simple problems. Minor variations in climate can destroy an entire animal species. Humans, when the temperature drops, can simply turn up the heat. This capacity for choice has led us near to disaster, but it has been and will continue to be our salvation.

In emergencies human beings can take automatic actions independent of intellect, although it may have been their intellect which indicated that they were "in extremis." At other times they will respond variably according to the relative merits and urgencies of the often contradictory conditional signals elicited. It is crucial, therefore, to understand the interplay of anger with some of these other emotions.

The most complicated and intricate linkage is the one between anger and fear. It is almost impossible to discuss anger without discussing fear. More important, it is almost impossible to locate either one of these emotions in an instance of human behavior without finding the other lurking in the background.

Recall the crucial developmental differences among animals. In lower forms capable only of perceiving a noxious and threatening influence, only irritability may exist. The vague and diffuse thrashing behavior is difficult to analyze in terms of its purposes. Is the wriggling, convulsing sea creature trying to destroy the stick that is prodding it or simply to escape from it? Perhaps whichever happens to be the more effective.

As the central nervous system develops and we ascend in complexity we see the emergence of emotions, the first great step in evolutionary adaptation. Possibly fear emerged first, and apart from anger, in small, helpless vegetarian creatures. In larger mating creatures, anger and aggression become central elements in intraspecies adaptation. The strong males move up the sexual ladder by intimidating the weaker males with their shows of aggression, thus dominating the breeding rights in the group and ensuring the enhancement of aggression in future generations.

For our purposes we can assume that fear and anger both emerged at roughly the same time. When danger appears both emotions are usually mobilized, although certain signs will trigger fear exclusively. Species have evolved to biologically "know" their enemies. This is not cognitive recognition. The field mouse does not say to himself anything equivalent to "Oh, my God, I think that is an owl silhouetted in the moonlight." The mouse is not capable of the kind of abstraction that would name a predator as an owl. Instead, the profile of an owl directly triggers a fear response in the mouse. As a result, paper owls can be used to frighten away their natural prey, and bird-lovers will paste a cutout of the profile of an owl or hawk on the surface of a window to keep small songbirds from damaging themselves by flying into it.

In those animals in which fear and anger are most automatically controlled, the signals for determining which emotion is more appropriate for each case are exact and precise. The smaller antagonist will trigger anger via some imprinting or recognition device. The larger or more dangerous antagonist will provoke fear. It does not take a highly developed forest animal to recognize that the appropriate response to fire is fear. No species that evolved with a fire-attacking impulse would be likely to survive. Again an intelligence must not be assumed in this situation. Certainly a choice ought not to be assumed. The behavior is a product of Darwinian adaptation. Those animals which are most keenly attuned to distinguishing between dangers that must be fled and dangers that ought to be fought are those which win the struggle for survival. Species will gradually emerge with finer and finer tuning devices for such immediate responses. This represents an alternative method for survival in a species that has not developed the capacity for judgment. The response of fish to changes in temperature, currents, oxygen levels and the like produce fine-tuning that is a splendid alternative to either emotion or intelligence.

Intelligence or judgment appeared in evolution well before the appearance of man. Even in lower animals there are ambiguous threats which must be tested and evaluated to determine whether fight or flight is appropriate. With *Homo sapiens* the relationship between fear and anger is even more complicated. Our imagination and our capacity for analytic reasoning permit us to anticipate the danger when there is no sensory awareness of it at all. We may have learned that in certain climates, in certain topography, at certain times of the year dangers are likely to occur in certain places. We may have remembered this from an encounter in the past. More important, we know it because of the unique and specific genetic endowment of the human species.

We are in a peculiar way a Lamarckian animal. In the debate between the followers of Lamarck and Mendel, the Lamarckian assumption that acquired characteristics were inherited eventually proved false. Mendel was right—with one possible and intriguing exception. The acquired characteristics of the human species *are* transmitted from generation to generation—not by genes, but through the means of culture: first through oral histories, then through the accretion of written knowledge. Modern biologists such as Theodosius Dobzhansky[18] have often pointed out that culture is in a sense a *genetic* mechanism in man, a product of our specific protoplasm and genes. We are a species capable of transmitting acquired characteristics through knowledge, language and foresight. It is not necessary, as it might be among lower animals, for each human being to rediscover the wheel. There is, of course, no lower animal that *could* discover the wheel.

This capacity to learn allows us to predict and anticipate. Anticipation can be troublesome in that it leaves us vulnerable to anticipating that which may never occur, but at this point it is necessary only to appreciate the enormous adaptive advantage inherent in the capacity for anticipation. We can make ourselves feel secure by reducing the number of emergencies that trigger fear/rage responses. The forests that are cleared and the stockades that are built around homesteads preclude the threatening emergence of a predatory animal or predatory person.

In addition, the increased warning time granted by crude lookout stations, telescopes or radar permits the easing of our first responses of anxiety and rage and the direction of our energies to more useful and cerebral methods of defense. There is no need for muscle tone to be improved by the excretion of chemicals and the impulses of neurons, since no physical power is needed to fire a rifle or press the button that drops the bomb from the relatively secure aircraft. A concept of military tactics may emerge. We begin to conceive of strategies of victory over larger time spans. Some battles are worth losing. Some victories can be deferred. The tactics of conflict become infinitely more complicated in a world of rationality.

Beyond this, other emotions, many possessed only by human beings, are capable of checking anger and buying time for more complicated forms of defense. Vengeance, retaliation, vendettas, the biding of time and the weaving of plots are specific human forms of aggression. Pride that is injured can command a peculiar, seemingly inexplicable action years later. Children are blown up by car bombs planted to avenge grievances of a hundred years before.

A clear head is necessary for delayed revenge and planned aggression. The physiological responses of fear and anger only get in the way. The emergency emotions are intended to short-circuit reasoning and facilitate an immediate response to the rampant aggressor at our throats. With intelligence, the aggressor rarely comes that close to our bodies. It is for precisely this reason that crime in the streets is now so terrifying. An immediate threat has become a new experience; it demands an immediacy of response that civilization has tended to block in us. Also, by its very atavistic nature it draws on our most primitive response mechanisms. This emergence of the jungle way of life brings out the beast that has never been completely tamed by our own biology. Fear and rage are brought back into the forefront of consciousness.

Pure rage, as I have suggested, may first be seen as primarily an intraspecies phenomenon. A male mammal will display signs of pure rage at the moment it senses a threat to its sexual rights over its harem or to the integrity of its territory. The emotion triggers behavior in the individual that serves the interests of the group. When the "enemy" is a competitive member of the herd, the show of anger can serve to frighten away the challenger, thereby avoiding a potentially dangerous conflict between two valuable members of the community.

This show of anger to induce physical fear in another is common among animals as a mechanism of social control that avoids battle, but does not occur often in interpersonal relationships because few of our power struggles are resolved by shows of force. Nonetheless, in subtle ways it is a powerful mechanism even in the city: people in the streets have trained themselves to walk tall, walk fast and walk tough; some affect aggressive facial expressions as they hustle their way down a dark city street. "Macho" signs of dress and decorum are used as intimidating or warning devices. People seem to yield right of way to the leather-jacketed, bearded and ill-kempt, prominently tattooed individual. It is an advertisement that may be as false as any other advertisement. But it is intended as an announcement of toughness, aggressiveness and belligerency and is perceived as such by many who will not run the risk of testing whether the article is that which it claims to be. People are often cowed when they sense that someone may lose his civilized veneer and become uncontrolled. We are so used to the containment of anger that aggressive displays are often effective devices of intimidation. I can think of at least two incidents in which calculated and feigned anger served its own purposes.

The first research that I did on social institutions required my visiting prisons.[19] I approached the prison authorities and guards with the same reserve, anxiety, politeness and caution I habitually use with any authority figure who controls my access to things I want. At the same time the prison guards saw me as an academic who was not "on their side" and who was potentially a trouble-maker. Predictably, they imposed a passive-aggressive resistance to all my courteous demands. Never mind the polite letters requesting certain prisoners at certain times for the spaced private interviews essential for my research. They had all been ignored. No such requests had ever been received; no permission had ever been granted. All my gentle protestations that "I think I had written in advance and was assured by the warden," and so on ad nauseam, resulted only in further delays, increased frustrations and new impediments.

Inevitably, the time came when I lost my temper—really lost my temper. By the second visit, after the third guard up the line of command assured me he didn't know who I was, that there had been no preparations for my arrival and no approval for my visit, I was reduced to the level of that street kid who still exists in even the most civilized middle-aged bourgeois gentleman. I launched into a tirade, couched in street language that advertised the passion and intent of the message. Rage prevailed where entreaty had failed.

From then on I always approached the prison with a surly, sullen, arrogant mien, particularly when faced by an unfamiliar guard. This was not a genuine anger. It was calculated as an expeditious way of getting my work done, and I was amazed at its effectiveness. In the prison environment of force and power, status and hierarchy are always clearly articulated. Symbols are clear and unambiguous. Life and death may depend on them. Badges and uniforms, billy clubs and manacles advertise the presence of the people in power. So do "sir" and "Mister." To fail to use these where their use is appropriate is to court disaster. But to use them where uncalled for is to announce your subservience. Softness is weakness, and politeness is softness. I was adjusting to the manners of the country.

I can recall another time when feigned anger served to mobilize anxiety and brought the kind of results one expects only in the jungle. It was a crowded scene in a suburban department store. In the preholiday rush my daughter and I were doing our shopping and chores. There is a kind of hysteria in women's-shoe departments that to a man seems different from the atmosphere of the depart-

ments with which he is familiar. The chaos seemed compounded by
the preholiday crowds. My daughter had to return a pair of shoes.
We were in a line of about five people waiting for returns or
exchanges, with half a dozen clerks running back and forth between
dozens of customers. We waited. After a while it became apparent
that selling was more important to the clerks than accepting returns. I asked one of them who would be able to take care of the
line. I got no response. I asked a second and got a surly response.
When the third came by I asked him if he could possibly call a floor
manager or someone in charge. The answer was one of those "Can't
you see we're busy?" responses.

What does one do in a situation like that? I looked at the others
in line and was given the pained, attempting-to-be-amused smiles
and shrugs that characterize the beaten masses confronting the im-
placable system. I had concluded that no one would pay attention
and was prepared to leave in defeat when the man in front of me
did the most incredible thing. This perfectly conventional man had
evidently been waiting, with his wife, at the edge of his patience.
Directly beside us was a pyramid of shoe boxes in a display, all
empty and all amusingly mounted to support one shoe on top. It
was a rainy day and he had an umbrella. He took the umbrella and
whacked the pyramid. Empty shoe boxes went flying all over.
Within moments, as if out of nowhere, salespeople, floor managers
and department heads appeared, asking him if there was anything
they could do to help. He announced that he had a pair of shoes to
return. They were eager to respond to his every need and satisfy his
every wish. He demurred, pointing out the two other people ahead
of him in the line, and despite their protestations patiently waited
his proper turn.

Their response was not out of concern for him, nor even out of
intellectual recognition that anyone so desperate for attention deserved or warranted it. They reacted from fear. Only crazy people
act the way he did in a public place. Crazy people are potentially
dangerous. The best way to handle them is to isolate or expel them
from the community—control them by banishment. One does not
reason with a crazy person; one gratifies his wish (if he had tried to
return a forty-year-old pair of filthy sneakers I suspect he would
have been accommodated) and gets him on his way.

The common intermingling of fear and anger makes separation of the emotions difficult. We do know that the emotions are different. We do know that they precipitate different kinds of behavior. Because of the possibilities of alternative defenses against a threat, these emotions tend to occur simultaneously. And even when a clear primacy of one exists the other is often present.

Psychoanalysts have confirmed this commingling, demonstrating that the explicit anxiety may be a cover for repressed rage, or vice versa—often to the chagrin of their patients who have adopted the conscious emotion as a defense against the unconscious and repressed ideas.

The concept of fear latent in anger is often more readily accepted than the idea of anger latent in fear. We know that we tend to be angry when we have been threatened by somebody. It does not matter what the source: public criticism by a stranger, an attack by a loved one, reading about a rape or mugging in our own middle-class neighborhood. In all these cases the manifest rage is related to an underlying fear. Some cases are more obvious than others, but generally the insights relative to unconscious fear are readily accepted.

At one time psychoanalysis did not acknowledge the primacy of fear. It was seen as a derivative of the sexual instinct, of primitive infantile desires. A basic principle of early Freudian psychoanalysis stated that "beneath every fear there is a wish." By this assumption, those most threatened by homosexuality will be those who fear their own homosexual impulses or are unsure, at least, of their own sexual identity. A psychoanalyst is likely to perceive a fear of exposure as a defense against an infantile desire to exhibit oneself. This mechanism does occur, although with less and less frequency as society grants respectability in the current marketplace of manners to all sorts of infantile sexual behavior. One need not fear one's exhibitionist impulses if one is allowed significant exposure in the public place with approbation or applause.

An unconscious desire for the "feared" thing lurks behind many fears. A person with paranoid jealousy is likely to be obsessed with personal desires for sexual adventure which frighten him. A desire or a wish is not the only or primary means of generating fear. Because of Freud's preoccupation with internal conflict it was to take him decades to "discover" primary fear, to acknowledge that fear was a "signal" of impending danger.[20]

Real fear, justified and warranted fear, primary fear—these are concepts which still unsettle many psychoanalysts who do not know quite what to do with such nonconflicted and straightforward emotions. Fear is a response to danger—neither more nor less. The danger can be derived from our own desires. It can also be a product of our own anger.

The latent anger in fear is often resisted. It is a more complicated mechanism. When we fear a nondangerous individual, it is almost always the destructive rage we feel toward that individual that we actually fear. When we fear an intimidating figure, we are still likely to find anger buried under the fear. The first response to the threatening individual will be both. The fact that we recognize our inadequacy to the task of destroying the threatening individual encourages the dominance of fear. The very fact that he has humiliated us by forcing us to recognize our inadequacy to his attack, to his presence and to his superior power will in itself generate anger. It is difficult to imagine a person frightened at this primitive level who does not conceal beneath his fear—or experience it concurrently—a rage at the threatening figure.

The rage is enhanced and compounded by two factors: first, that it must be suppressed acknowledges our inferiority to the aggressor; and second, the very impounding of the emotion disrupts the homeostatic mechanism which might have diminished it had we been free to release the anger. Usually this anger is so close to the surface, the rage not repressed but being simply impounded, that most of us are completely aware of the coexistence of the secondary emotion contained within the prevailing mood of the dominant emotion.

What is more troublesome to recognize is that *unconscious* anger may be the actual *cause* of the fear. One sees this at its most heightened form in certain kinds of sexual impotence.

Impotent men are often simply frightened by women. They see the vagina as an instrument of castration, an open mouth ready to destroy or diminish the potency which they symbolically vest in their phallus. This phenomenon has been termed *vagina dentata* ("toothed"). Fantasies of a destructive vagina occur frequently in the dreams and fantasies of men with potency problems. Such men are particularly prone to a condition known as premature ejaculation. Here ejaculation occurs at the moment of, or immediately preceding, penetration, thus protecting the phallus from prolonged contact with the instrument of castration. But an alternative source of fear of women derives from the view of the phallus itself as an instrument of destruction—or at least dominance. What the impotent man may be fearing is the release of his own rage and destructiveness toward women. Intercourse is seen as a lacerating attack on the woman. The "absence" of a penis in the woman is seen as a proof and sign of castration. Each attempt at intercourse can be viewed as a symbolic repetition of the castrative assault.

Of course, women raised in our male-dominant society are subject to precisely the same fantasies. They can fear the penis as an instrument of castration and humiliation, or they can be frightened by their own rage at men, seeing intercourse as a means of disarming the man and reducing him. Because these more primitive feelings are repressed, all the individual will be aware of is the fear. A suggestion that maybe their own anger is frightening them is dismissed, or treated with angry contempt.

One need not accept any of these specific constructs to acknowledge the reciprocity that exists between fear and anger. A wise and useful exercise is the examination of one's own fears in terms of potential anger, and vice versa. This is one of the few "self-help" tips of real potential value. Parents particularly are aware of how often their anger toward a child is a product of some fear. Exposing the fear may avert an inappropriate show of anger.

Much of the discussion antecedent to this has dealt with the survival of the individual. Fear and rage are the emergency emotions biologically designed to support individual survival. But *Homo sapiens* is not technically or biologically a true individual. He is an obligate social animal, in the sense that people are as necessary for his survival as are air, water and nutrients. Although we are not bound to each other physically, as in a colony of coral, there are psychological, sociological and developmental bonds that make us something like a colonial animal. Group survival is enhanced by mitigation of anger and fear through emotions of guilt, shame and pride.

A large body of research supports the proposition that were we capable of finding some artificial means of supporting the *biological* needs of the developing child while depriving him of involvement with people, that which would develop would be less than human.[21] We have seen the damage done when clean and efficient institutions were regarded as generally superior to somewhat sloppy and less efficient foster homes. Children who had been institutionalized under the most sterile of conditions while deprived of sufficient human contact failed to develop certain essential aspects of human-hood. The most fragile traits were those most necessary for social living—that is, the capacity to form loving attachments, to ex-perience true guilt, to have a developed and mature conscience. Nowhere is the interplay between biological directives and en-vironmental facilitation more beautifully demonstrated. Genetic codes in areas of such complicated behavior are always incomplete signals which demand environmental cooperation for fulfillment. Human contact, association with one's own kind, not only is essen-tial for sustaining the life of the developing creature but is necessary to endow that creature with those special features we identify as human.

The wisdom of the body must somehow or other allow for our obligation to the species as a whole. There must be biological drives that limit and challenge the concern for individual survival in the service of the larger community. In our biology there must exist built-in devices which support and testify to that which we have intellectually forgotten in an age of rampant individualism—that the well-being of the individual is precarious if the social unit is unbalanced. We cannot serve individual liberty and individual right by destroying the community. Our physiology has to have been "designed" with this in mind in order for a species as pecu-liarly interdependent as ours to survive.

Well before our ancestors were sufficiently sophisticated to re-alize the relationship of copulation to the eventual birth, the child was protected by the adults in the community. The kinship be-tween a father and child is a less apparent biological fact than the kinship between a mother and child. Fatherhood must have been a relatively late development in the conceptual life of our species, probably only after the introduction of animal husbandry. Nonetheless, the species survived. The infant was rarely seen as fit food for a hungry adult male of the tribe during periods of famine and deprivation. The evidence for an essential nurturing and caring biology in *Homo sapiens* is too extensive to be elaborated here, but the evidence exists.

Beyond the dependency apparatus that allows us to empathize with the weak and helpless, other feelings—guilt and shame—are built within us as part of an emotional repertoire that limits a selfish pursuit of individual survival. These operate as automatically as fear and anger, but unfortunately are more vulnerable to abuse. We must remember that the variability and adaptability that are our species' strongest support in times of adversity also make us capable of modifying our nature in negative ways. We can, if we try hard enough, destroy the compassion and undermine the identity which serve group survival.

The primary emotions of cohesiveness are guilt, shame and pride, the essential components of human conscience. These are specifically human emotions. It is unlikely that lower mammals experience guilt, although many of us are anthropomorphically inclined to endow our pets with this emotion. Guilt should not be confused with guilty fear—which is fear, neither more nor less, initiated by the knowledge of having done something wrong for which one can expect punishment. The emotion is fear, and the evasion or avoidance of punishment is greeted with relief in the presence of this emotion. True guilt is an excruciatingly painful emotion. Guilt sees us as both the one to be punished and the punisher. It is ourselves against ourselves. Or more exactly, ourselves against an image of ourselves the way we would like to be. It is the violation or failure of that image which produces the sense of guilt. Of course, the image must be there: we must first have developed a sense of ideal behavior. We must have incorporated figures with which to identify and introjected a value system appropriate for such identity. My favorite definition of guilt is that of an eighteenth-century minister: "Nothing else but the trouble arising in our mind from our consciousness of having done contrary to what we are barely perswaded [*sic*] was our Duty."[22] Guilt is, as Paul Ricoeur has said, a way "of putting ourselves before an internalized tribunal which measures our offense, pronounces our condemnation and inflicts the punishment. It is an expression of our disappointment in ourself. We are anguished by our personal failure that we are not better than we should be." [23]

Certain connections between rage and guilt are obvious. When rage is directed inappropriately, we are likely to experience a painful sense of guilt. Guilt then will either check the expression of the rage or limit it. This is an experience too common for the reader not to have shared in it. Returning from a frustrating, humiliating day at work, a parent or spouse will find any excuse to explode at the safer but more vulnerable people around him rather than at the indifferent and threatening authority who generated the rage. An infraction that would be ignored under normal circumstances produces a sudden and violent outburst. The inflicting of pain on those close in emotional affinity and shared destiny is for the most part likely to produce an agonizing sense of guilt which will serve both to abort the action and to institute the rectifying behavior that will restore the sense of love. When this unfortunately fragile guilt mechanism is absent we get the child abusers, the wife beaters, the sadists.

Those who are susceptible to strong guilt feelings are often shocked at how readily guilt can be precipitated and how all-pervasive and irrational it can be. Hypersensitive feelers of guilt can torture themselves with small wrongs they have committed. It is true that many can suffer from inappropriate guilt, and our guilt can be manipulated as a controlling device by those around us. Nonetheless, the trend of modern-day psychology books to see guilt as a maladaptive emotion has been a disaster. It is a product of the same culture that traditionally overvalues individual needs over group survival.

Guilt, then, is a check on aggression and, along with pride, a limiting factor on rampant individualism, at least in the moral sphere. Ironically, the very painful nature of guilt which proves so effective in impelling us toward behavior that will obviate it also leads to a mechanism that subverts its intentions and purposes. That is the conversion of guilt into anger. To feel anger is less painful than to feel guilt. This defensive maneuver, which I have called the "hot-potato game," is an almost universal element in marital lives. It causes more unnecessary discord than any other single complex of emotion, with the probable exception of sexual anger and fear.

Not all things that go wrong are someone's fault. Many things that do go wrong could have been avoided with prescience or planning, but just as many could not possibly have been anticipated. I am not at all sure why we start with the assumption that somebody must be to blame for everything. It may be part of the general denigration of the concept of chance in our culture. Nonetheless, the first reaction when something goes awry is to wonder whose fault it is. The next reaction is to try to protect against the assignment of fault to ourselves.

In ambiguous situations where no one may be to blame, or where we vaguely may assume some guilt, the hot potato is passed on. We do this by quickly assigning (before it can be assigned to us) the responsibility for the selection of the dreadful play; the incorrect road back home; the date of the picnic on which a torrential rain occurred. It was your idea; it must be your fault: at least, it was surely not mine. We preempt the role of the innocent.

Even when the fault is clearly one's own, if one can find some elliptical sequence of causal agents leading back to another rather than to oneself, it is taken with relief. I am careless in my driving; I cut a corner too sharply and bash in my right fender. I am relieved and delighted if the purpose of my trip is an errand for my wife. Why? It was still my preoccupation or my carelessness that caused the accident. But now I have established a causal relationship that connects my wife with the unfortunate and expensive accident. I would not have taken the car out of the garage if I were not on an errand for her. Therefore a necessary, if not sufficient, cause of the accident can be assigned to my wife. I would like to think that my dignity and intelligence would not allow me to use such meretricious means of evading guilt. I know this to be untrue. My first response, immediately after a sickening swell of guilt, will too often be anger. In my better moments and in my more rational periods the anger will be quickly dissipated by chagrin at the embarrassed recognition of my childish defensive maneuver and a reawakened sense of fairness. But generally speaking, given the choice between feeling guilty, with the sickening sense of diminution it produces, and feeling angry, we will elect anger, at least as our first response.

The maladaptive nature of this is twofold. If attacked, particularly unjustly, the spouse or loved person is likely to respond in turn with anger. If we had presented her with our own pain and guilt, the nurturing quality of the relationship might have been encouraged, thereby eliciting the love that dissipates guilt by reassuring us that we are loved, therefore lovable and worthy. Instead, by instituting this silly game designed to protect ourselves from guilt, we invite attack. We generate anger and abort the nurturing quality inherent in love relationships. It converts a reliable and necessary ally into a temporary "enemy."

Guilt can thus be an alternative to anger, when we acknowledge our own responsibility for the damaging incident that endangered us; it can set a limit to the amount of anger we will feel or express; but we can then convert the guilt into anger to relieve ourselves from its pain. The rapidity of the alternation of these emotions, and the capacity to generate them simultaneously, as if they were musical chords, make the psychological and biological study of emotion extraordinarily difficult.

I have singled out guilt for a paradigmatic discussion. Shame and humiliation, or any of half a dozen other emotions, can equally modify anger. One can follow the emotions of shame and humiliation and see how they too will interact with and place checks on anger. Even people without a clearly defined or strongly honed sense of guilt may have a sense of shame. To be exposed and humiliated in the public eye is an agony for almost all. It explains the effectiveness of open rebuke as an instrument of punishment and a means of socially controlling behavior.

"Shame," as Aristotle said, "is a mental picture of disgrace in which we shrink from the disgrace itself and not from its consequences."[24] Obviously shame serves in the most direct way the purpose of preserving the community. The tendency in the last thirty years to cast all moral issues in terms of legal rights makes it seem as if morality can be enforced only through the state or its agencies. We do not refrain from certain antisocial behavior simply because it is against the law and we would be punished for it. That is never the only limitation on our behavior. I do not refrain from urinating in the classroom because it is against the law to do so. For that matter, I do not—or try not to—pass gas in that same classroom, even though I suspect in most states there is no law against it. The reasons for avoiding both of these activities are more complicated than simply fear of punishment. There are shame, pride in my own deportment, humiliation, consideration for my friends and fear of the ridicule that might follow.

The complicated interplay of emotions and constraint that are woven together into the elaborate design of social manners and public decorum is reinforced and supported by more than fear of prosecution. To trip an old lady in beating her to the only cab available may be construed by a judge as assault, but I do not think that that is the chief constraint which keeps most of us from knocking down old ladies.

Shame allows the community and its standards to be joined with the more personally derived emotions of guilt and pride in shaping our behavior. The values of the community then become, along with the more idiosyncratic standards of our family, incorporated into that ego ideal which will serve as a standard. It will be the ideal against which actual behavior will be compared, and will determine whether such behavior generates pride, or shame, or guilt. This incorporation of community values explains ethnic and regional variations. While generalizations in this area can be treacherous, most of us acknowledge that approved standards of public behavior differ from culture to culture, country to country and time to time.

Heterogeneous communities often experience more problems with public behavior because of the confusion and conflict that arise when the internalized standards with which we were raised are different from those among which we are now residing. This also presents a dilemma when we are in a period of radical transition from one set of community values to another. Many women pursuing the feminist ideals of our time are painfully aware that much of the value system which they have unequivocally rejected continues to operate within them from their past training and indoctrination.

71

Despite their intellectual commitment to a feminist equality, they still carry these abandoned and despised biases from a past from which few are ever capable of completely freeing themselves.

If guilt is the negative fuel that stokes our conscience, pride is its opposite, affirmative emotion. Both can limit selfish anger. Pride has multiple uses and may be understood by different people in its different contexts. Pride can be the sense of our head held high in public, secure in our knowledge of the positive judgment of those around us. In this sense pride is the antithesis not of guilt but of shame and humiliation. In either case, pride is an important positive reinforcement toward good behavior. Those of us with developed consciences will be disappointed at our selfish actions and proud of our self-denials in service of the public good. And pride is its own reward. It feels good to do good. The fact that doing good feels good has become the sophistry of generations of undergraduates who have used this as an argument to prove that all behavior is selfish. The argument is that since it makes one feel good, the person doing good is behaving as selfishly as the person who greedily takes all benefits for himself. It is not worth the time for refutation—except to point out that we are free to define goodness as residing in that person who takes pleasure in unselfish acts, and evil in that person who takes pleasure in selfish acts. The moral world remains intact with either set of definitions. I simply prefer to call the one selfish and the other unselfish, allowing normative judgments to stand there.

Fear and anger, then, are bound to guilt and shame, pride and love, joy and righteous indignation, compassion and selflessness. The response patterns elicited by the complex and differing combinations of emotions in turn elicit vastly different scenarios of behavior. These are often mechanically and automatically controlled, bypassing cognition.

Any solution that attempts to directly alter physiological mechanisms for generating the emergency emotions must acknowledge the tendency for fear and rage to be generated in combination with antagonistic emotions to control them. In attempting to restrict the outpouring of a destructive anger, we must be careful not to obliterate those emotions essential for community living. How in the world are we to separate anger from the fear that will always be an essential part of all survival mechanisms? How are we to separate it from guilt and shame when these are the mediators of the social good? How are we to separate anger from righteous indignation— which is simply the same emotion now ennobled by the context in which it arises? It is a complication that must be kept clearly in mind as we enter the age of biological and pharmacological under- standing of emotions. We are not yet at that point where we can actively "operate" on our emotion-producing mechanisms; but we are not far from that technological point either. We already have tranquilizers and sedatives that dull anxiety and agitation and some that seem to deal directly with anger. While we await this technical development, we must examine less exotic means of grappling with this problem in adaptation.

We have other alternatives. Methods of handling anger have evolved and been designed and even prescribed well before we even conceived of physiological controls of emotion. Different cultures and different states in the past have established control measures to limit rampant or destructive self-serving impulses which might threaten either the individual himself or the integrity of the com- munity. But there have been historical and cultural variations as to what were considered appropriate amounts of anger and what were considered the proper means of expressing it. We are beginning to question the reliability of our contemporary attitudes. It is worth examining some of the traditional control methods of the past.

5. The Proper Uses of Anger

Compared with that of other life forms, the history of humanity is short, probably less than two million years. Within that brief history, the period that can be called the age of civilization and culture is but a fraction.

In prehistoric times the basic social unit was a family or a small clan, and the rules of survival were simple. Space, shelter, food, fire and biological continuity—these were the necessities of life, and any threat to these was a threat to the individual, the family or the sense of biological survival. The threats were essentially physical: a man with a stone, perhaps later the man with the axe, a predatory animal, a landslide, a physical impediment to a goal. All the threats to survival could be defined in physical terms. The two great devices of survival for the adult were flight and fight. The physiology of fear subserved the first, and the physiology of anger was a reasonable preparation for the assault.

With civilization, the rules changed and threats to survival became more complicated. It was inevitable that various cultures would debate the propriety, the purpose and the very value of such an emotion as anger. The role of anger in human behavior and the proper attitudes toward personal anger occupied the scholars of the Old Testament, as well as Mencius, Plato, Aristotle, Seneca and others. The great God Jehovah in the Old Testament was capable of great wrath. Yet the Old Testament is not clear or consistent as to how one should appraise this anger in God. The Old Testament God is, after all, not a model; His nature is not intended to be aspired to, as is that of the Christ of the New Testament. "I am that I am" announces a mystery and uniqueness that make evident the *hubris,* if not impossibility, of emulation. God's actions are neither defendable or fully understandable. Moses, who had suffered a lifetime to serve his people and bring them to the Promised Land, was denied that privilege as punishment for his anger by that very God who raged at those same inconstant people.

Still, the heroes of the Old Testament were imbued with fire and rage, from the psychotic rage of Saul to the unpredictable rage of David to the justifiable rage of Jeremiah. Their heroism remains undiminished, really enhanced, by their human qualities of frustration, annoyance, irritability and temper—all dimensions of anger. Perhaps it was not Moses' anger that brought down such heartless punishment but rather the destruction of the holiest aspect of the Jewish religion, the Tablets of the Law. The Law is the venerated foundation of Jewish morality. This ambiguity of the Jews toward the expression of anger is testament to a philosophy that, while respecting the individual, places the ultimate burden of morality on the survival of a people chosen by God to sustain His Law. Group survival in a humanistic democracy always demands an agonizing compromise between the rights of the individual—including the rights to his emotional life—and the needs of social order.

The Greeks had more problems and less ambiguity about human anger. With the rise of Apollo as a model, temperance in all things became the touchstone of the good and decent life. Plato first suggested that anger is a disbalance; this understanding comes amazingly close to the modern physiological theory of homeostatic anger. Plato assumed that all varieties of ill temper came from melancholia. Brashness and cowardice were produced by the wandering through the body of "acid and briny flegm and other bitter bilious humours" [1]—a chemical theory before its time.

It remained for Aristotle, with his strong biological roots, to enunciate an attitude toward anger which acknowledged its value.

He neither condemned it out of hand nor allowed it full reign. As with all other emotions, he praised the median in the expression and use of anger. He was certainly no Christian arguing that the good man must abandon all his rights to negative passion, must love his enemy and turn the other cheek. "Those who do not show anger at things that ought to arouse anger are regarded as fools; so too if they do not show anger in the right way, the right time or at the right person." [2]

Anger is defined by Aristotle as "an impulse attended with pain to avenge an undeserved slight openly manifested toward ourselves or friends." It is in every way a legitimate emotion. There is no suggestion that it is antagonistic to, or a denial of, our rational selves. The only constrictions on anger are that it be "at the right time, place and right degree and duration."

Seneca offered the first well-articulated expression in Western culture of the idea that anger is the foe of reason. Intriguingly, Seneca starts his argument by denying a capacity in animals to feel *any* emotion. Therefore, ironically, though anger is the foe of reason, it is born only where reason dwells. He defines anger as the desire for avenging injury. He believes that it has cost the human race "more than any plague." "Man," Seneca says, "is born for mutual help, anger for mutual destruction." Anger is against the true nature of man. [3] He refuses to acknowledge any useful role for anger in human affairs and confronts Aristotle directly, insisting that even during war anger is useless. He cautions against it at its earliest appearance. Since reason becomes contaminated when mingled with passion, "the best course is to reject at once the first incitement to anger, to resist even its small beginnings and to take pains to avoid falling into anger." [4]

Aristotle had argued that certain passions serve as armament. This was a mark of Aristotle's extraordinary intuition in biological matters. In a day when no one truly understood physiology, Aristotle intuitively sensed the "arming" mechanism of the emotions. Seneca, in rejecting any value for anger, anticipated a Christian dualism, pitting the animal nature of man against its "higher" and nobler spiritual and rational self. In refuting the concept of passions as useful weapons, Seneca denied the value of Aristotle's analogy, arguing that these "arms," unlike actual weapons, fight under their own command, thus are not possessed by the person, but rather possess him. "Anger I say has this great fault—it refuses to be ruled."[5]

This concept of possession by one's own emotions is an essential aspect of the distrust of emotion that runs as a constant thread through civilized thought up to the very present. Seneca concluded that nature had given man adequate equipment for survival in his reason. Reason could be trusted because it considers only the question at issue, while anger is moved by "trifling things that lie outside the case."[6]

In the thirteenth century, Thomas Aquinas continued Aristotle's argument defending the legitimacy and usefulness of anger. Being a gifted and brilliant observer of human nature, he offered new insights into the nature of the emotion.[7] He pointed out, for example, that anger has no opposite. Many scholars, even today, still continue to juxtapose love and anger as though they were polar phenomena. They are not, for we are much more likely to be angry with those we love than with anyone else. If there is any "opposite" to anger (and there is not, in a truly polar sense) one would have to say it would be indifference—which is also precisely the opposite of love.

The complexity of emotions tends to be underestimated. While occasionally occurring in pure form, emotions more often come commingled in an amalgam or medley of feelings that are often contradictory. Think of the ambivalence and confusion when we become enraged at the child we love for putting himself into a position of danger. Aquinas recognized this complexity, observing that anger is even contradictory within itself, and therefore a complex passion in its purest form. The object of anger is evil in the sense that one sorrows over an injustice or slight to one's self; its purpose is good in the sense that one seeks revenge for the injury done to one's self. To some Aquinas may seem singularly un-Christian in his insistence on the rightness of revenge.

Aquinas also believed that anger is almost exclusively an emotion directed toward another person. When one seems angry with a group, it is only insofar as the group is considered a unity; and one can be angry at inanimate objects only metaphorically, insofar as they seem animated at the moment the anger is generated.

Of course he acknowledged that anger could be a vice if it were habitual and not justifiable or under "right reason." The virtue of prudence must always be present for anger to be justified. Prudence not only guides the correct use of anger but can serve to prevent or curb anger when it is aroused quickly and not under the control of reason. Nonetheless, when anger is justified it can be good. Indeed, Aquinas was prepared to go further. Failure to use anger under just circumstances could be a sin of omission. There are times when we are morally mandated to be angry.

From the classic period into the modern era the debate has continued. Aristotle and Seneca both have their followers. At the turn of the century, with the discovery of the "sciences of the mind," the debate took on the aura of a search for scientific truth. An attempt was made to bring analytic methods and sometimes even the empiric tools of science to bear on the question of human anger.

Alexander Bain (1888), agreeing with Aristotle, held that anger was a "desire to inflict pain" and, along with righteous indignation, had its place. He proposed even further that there is "a pleasure of malevolence" present in anger. He used as an example "the noble rage" of Homer's Achilles.[8]

Yet his view of human nature was hardly flattering. Anger, according to Bain, has four ingredients, and while most of us would not see them as either the exclusive or the essential ingredients, many would, with a certain chagrin, recognize aspects of their own behavior in these early descriptions.

First, Bain states that the frenzied excitement generated by anger desperately seeks some way to find activity to give vent to this energy. He follows this thought with three comments about the pleasure of venting anger: the sight of bodily affliction and suffering seems to be a mode of sensual and sensuous pleasure; the "pleasure of power" is pandered to; there is a satisfaction in preventing further pain to ourselves by inducing fear of us.

Another writer of this time, A. Riboat,[9] agreed with Bain that the pleasure of anger resides in fascination at the sight of bodily affliction and suffering. He went further and suggested that within us is a destructive instinct plus an instinct toward domination. No longer was anger simply a mechanism ensuring our survival. Somehow or other it was extended to the point that our survival was now to be viewed in terms of the destruction, or at least the domination, of others.

Joining these experts was R. F. Richardson, who felt strongly that one should have a working residue of anger on tap for when it is needed. "Good healthy resentment is at times a good thing and should be kept alive." [10] Richardson quoted Goethe as saying, "With most of us the requisite intensity of passion is not forthcoming without an element of resentment, and common sense and careful observation will, I believe, confirm the opinion that few people who amount to anything are without a good capacity for hostile feeling upon which they draw freely when they need it." [11]

In the same mode of reasoning G. M. Stratton took the argument for the justification of anger one step further and gave it moral sanction. "Anger, we may say, is an achievement in mental progress. Its coming is preceded by an angerless existence, but when once it comes it is never permitted to disappear. The better kinds of animal life depend upon its powerful aid." [12] He continued, ". . . we owe much of our social life within the state to indignation, resentment, jealousy and revenge. These come to the help of the family and commerce and class and the institutions of law." [13] While Stratton fell short of stating that anger and pugnacity are at the source of virtue and moral life, he insisted that they help to maintain them by stating that the bellicose passions fight as readily for virtue as they do for vice.

These writings of some sixty to one hundred years ago are a revelation to those of us in the psychological field who have been aware of the failure of the modern world of psychology to pay serious attention to the emotions. Stratton clearly understood that anger implied a serious relationship between the angry person and the object of his wrath. "Anyone who enrages me has already drawn from me a sincere expression of regard." [14] He was also no unilateral disarmer. "The man of goodwill must be prepared to be angry as long as others are prepared." [15]

For Stratton, the solution was clear. Since anger serves a reasonable adaptive purpose and can be seen as an instrument of the moral life it should not be eradicated but rather controlled through proper training. "There would seem, then, to be both the possibility and the need of bringing our anger response into the service of the interests who deserve to be supreme, and in particular of making pugnacity obedient to goodwill." [16] We must train ourselves "in the schooling of our native passions, in giving them their master and their task, and making anger a true servant of goodwill . . ." [17]

In contrast to these writers who clearly felt the adaptive value of anger there were those who, like Seneca, drew distinct lines between passion and reason. The rationalists and the optimists felt that self-will could and must control the passions. Perhaps the best spokesman for this position was Horace Fletcher. He started with the premise that anger is an evil passion and that "the elimination of the evil passions is entirely possible." With a title that was made to order for the best-seller lists of our own day—*Menticulture, the A.B.C.'s of True Living*—Fletcher spelled it all out.

All the evil passions are traceable to one of two roots. Anger is the root of all aggressive passions; worry is the root of all cowardly passions. Envy, spite, revenge, impatience, annoyance, selfishness, prejudice and the like are all phases of anger. Jealousy, fear, the belittling of self, blues and all introspective forms of depression are the children of worry. Anger and worry are the most unprofitable conditions known to man. While they are in possession of the mind both mental and physical growth are suspended. Anger and worry are "thieves" that steal precious time and energy from life. They are the most potent form of self-abuse. They do not stimulate to any good end. Anger and worry are no more necessary than other passions civilized man has learned to control. [18]

Fletcher believed that in order to achieve happiness we must merely emancipate ourselves from anger and worry. He was also quite confident that we could achieve this end. With the scientific optimism that characterized the turn of the century, he advises that "anger and worry are creations of the mind that can be dispelled by the same power that gave them birth." [19]

Now, what can we learn from Sigmund Freud, that giant of modern-day psychology whose creative forces were at their peak at the turn of the century? Amazingly, Freud has very little to say about anger. He was aware of the importance of feelings in everyday life, and he certainly placed them in a central role in the therapeutic process. "We remain on the surface as long as we are dealing only with memories and ideas. What is alone of value in mental life is rather the feelings. . . . ideas are repressed only because they are associated with the release of feelings which ought not to occur." [20] But it was with ideas and instincts that he was really fascinated. Freud was concerned with conflict, particularly internal conflict. If there was one emotion that was allowed entry into Freud's psychoanalytic theory it was anxiety. But even then, for the first forty years of his productive life he saw anxiety as a peripheral and derivative phenomenon. It was the sexual appetite that drove our behavior and the corruption of the sexual instinct that led to all neuroses.

Failure to deal with anger and aggression was one of the major deficiencies in early Freudian theory. As a theoretician who placed the Oedipal conflict at the center of all problems Freud cannot have been unaware of competition, but he never adequately incorporated the dynamic role of the emotions into the theory of psychoanalysis.

This failure on Freud's part was to have a shattering effect on the studies of emotion. Modern psychology was dominated by two powerful schools of thought: dynamic psychology and behaviorism. Dynamic psychology, with its emphasis on motivation, conflict and the unconscious, was a direct derivative of Freud. It took its focus, direction, content and, until pathetically recently, its very language from Freud. Since Freud dealt only peripherally with emotions, conventional psychoanalysis also ignored them.

Behaviorism—from I. P. Pavlov through J. B. Watson to B. F. Skinner—empirically and often slavishly devoted itself to observing behavior. As a school, the behaviorists had contempt for something so impalpable, so *unmeasurable,* as feelings, and under Skinner's direction they refused to grant any validity to the concept of feeling. Physiology and behavior were all. Because of their obsession with statistics and data, the leading behaviorists were infatuated with the pigeon and the rat. They were spending little time with people. They may have been encouraged by the fact that during this same period psychoanalysts were forgetting their roots in empirical medical science. Nonetheless, pigeons and rats have very limited emotional experience and a very limited capacity to articulate what little they do experience.

The field of emotions was abandoned to the occasional lone eccentric academic who wandered through. With little ongoing research, the public messages on anger and its expression were generally delivered by untutored and unknowledgeable purveyors of self-help.

Furthering the neglect of emotion was the absence of any spirited moral philosophical interest. In the modern period, philosophy too seemed bored with human beings and their problems. Philosophy was intimidated by science, and imitated its techniques. Analysis and method were all. Good and evil; right and wrong; the nature of man—these were part of a normative philosophy that had no cachet, no currency in the modern philosophical exchanges.

How one handles one's anger was relegated to the domain of manners and mores, unguided by any theoretical justifications. With the rise of rampant individualism, and the cult of health and self-expression, of course one "did one's own thing." The concept of a group "thing" (let alone an acknowledgment of the existence of a group) never did develop. You were simply encouraged to express yourself—all over your neighbor if necessary.

This movement took whatever rationale it required from a misreading of early Freud, and an exaggerated fear of suppressed anger and its potential internal consequences, while ignoring the very real external danger inherent in expressing anger. In his first speculation in *Studies in Hysteria* (1895), Freud postulated with his coauthor, Josef Breuer,[21] that neurosis was due to the accidental encapsulation of an emotion which failed to be discharged. Much of the cathartic, howling confrontation theories so popular today derives from a sloppy reading of this early Freudian writing. Freud spent most of his life modifying the concept of "encapsulation," and very early gave up the idea that simple catharsis solved anything.

The early psychoanalytic concept of a damaging effect of dammed-up emotion received support from the burgeoning field of psychosomatic medicine, with its emphasis on the contributing role

of emotion, particularly anger, in symptom formation. To understand the link between anger and illness, it is necessary to return
once more to the field of physiology. The debate over the values of
expressed anger versus repressed anger draws many conclusions,
often false ones, from the new knowledge.

Most physiological systems tend to operate according to the
principle of homeostasis. The principle was introduced to physiology by the great nineteenth-century French physiologist Claude
Bernard.[22] It is a notion that has remained central to modern physiology and has contributed immensely to forming our modern concept of disease and therapeutics.

Homeostasis assumes a steady state of balance in the basic systems that control our body functions. Any condition which disturbs
this "steady state" will automatically initiate countermeasures
within the physiology of the animal to restore the balance. The
degree to which our bodies are kept in a constant state of optimal
functioning would astound a lay public inexcusably ignorant of its
own biology.

One readily grasped example of a homeostatic mechanism involves the control of body temperature. Most chemical reactions of
the body operate best at a certain fixed temperature. That temperature is 98.6 degrees Fahrenheit, and independently of the heat
outside or the cold north winds, we manage to maintain this temperature. Certain rare functions may operate better at different
temperatures. For example, sperm require a somewhat lower temperature, being destroyed at 98.6 degrees. The sperm are, therefore, contained in testicles in a scrotal sac that hangs "outside" the
body. There the sperm can be manufactured and stored at temperatures below the body level. A strange phenomenon noticed by
most men is that when the room or the weather is hot or when
bodily heat has been generated by exercise, or in a hot shower, the
scrotum tends to expand, lowering the testes away from the body.
Conversely, when a man emerges from a shower shivering cold, the
scrotal sac contracts, tucking the testes up close for body warmth.
This is a simple example of homeostatic control, operating without
a need for cooperation, or even awareness, from the "higher" brain
—the cortex.

Similarly, when the body is invaded by infectious organisms, an increase in the metabolic rate is helpful to overcome the invaders. Body temperature is elevated. We have a "fever." Fever, which at one time was seen as sickness, can now be understood as a reparative maneuver to help in curing the disease, the actual disease being the invasion of the body by the microbes.

These examples both involve maintaining appropriate body temperature. In that sense we can understand them by thinking of a home thermostat. We set a thermostat at an ideal temperature for our comfort—68 degrees. When the temperature falls below that point, a circuit is closed (precisely as though a switch had been manually turned on) which then starts up the furnace. The temperature gradually rises, and when it reaches the ideal level the circuit is broken and the furnace goes off. This is a simple, physical homeostatic device. Those in the body are infinitely more complicated, involving multiple variables mediated by a combination of physical and chemical devices. These mechanisms control electrolyte and fluid balance, sugar levels in the blood, circulating endocrines, hormone levels that influence fertility and menstruation—all the vital balances of the body.

Emotions also operate according to such homeostatic regulation. This mechanism, however, was fixed in our biological system millions of years before anything remotely resembling modern culture existed. And for millions of years it served us well. But the civilization that we have developed in just the past trifling few thousand years is rapidly encroaching on the fixed assumptions of this system and is raising serious questions about "the wisdom of the body."

This has been expressed well by Sterling and Eyer. "It is the common view the body's physiological systems are held 'constant' by simple, regulatory feedback loops. This belief in 'internal constancy' leads physicians to view unusual elevations or depressions of body metabolites or hormones as 'inappropriate' and to combat these changes by interventions with drugs or surgery. [But] many of these metabolic alternations make sense as part of the individual's overall process of coping with the environment and . . . the metabolic changes are merely reflections of the brain's control over physiology. Both the coping and the accompanying metabolic changes are *entirely* appropriate to the social environment. If anything is inappropriate, it is the social environment which both stimulates and demands unremitting coping."[23]

In part they are right. It may be that society has created for us an environment which no longer satisfies our basic needs, which places us in constant stress. But it is more complicated. The true nature of distress has changed. The environment that is most critical to *Homo sapiens* is not always the world he lives in. More important to him is the world he *thinks* he lives in. Our brain has developed a capacity to create for us a world of our own making and imagination. Very few of us live in the real world. We live in the world of our perceptions, and those perceptions differ dramatically according to our personal experiences. We may perceive danger where there is none. If the distortion is severe enough we may think we are living among enemies even while surrounded by friends. We may feel deprived in the face of abundance.

The actual social environment rarely generates the anguish in our lives except in extreme cases. Individuals are capable of living in great privation under circumstances of extreme hardship, pain and misery, and suffer little in the way of psychological or psychosomatic damage. Yet at other times, surrounded by the symbols and rewards of affluence and success they may suffer the envy, the hunger and the rage of feeling deprived.

In bourgeois America it is not the social environment which generally stimulates and demands unremitting coping. It is the psychological or psychosocial environment. We are often tragic figures who like Don Quixote fight battles that exist only in our own perception, attacking monsters that exist only in our own minds, converting neutral phenomena into dangers to survival. This is because we experience an existential *Angst* so profound we dare not face it. Since we feel we cannot cope with the broad, pervasive existential threats to our life, identity and happiness, we manufacture simpler ones to justify our rage. We cannot acknowledge, let alone rage at, the inevitability of our death or the joylessness of our existence. Who knows the sum total of contributions to the anger of either the cabby or the jaywalker?

We find false causes for our anger in order to have the gratification of attacking something, and it is not a totally purposeless exercise. The irrational attack will at least complete the homeostatic cycle and turn off the anger-generating mechanism. But since the true threat remains unaltered it will continue to send warning signals, and we will continue to initiate the emergency responses of fear and anger.

The mechanisms for initiating rage reactions are located in the midbrain. They are "old-brain" functions and as such part of our animal heritage from earlier evolution. Most of these arousal patterns are therefore surprisingly similar in all higher mammals. It is this which has encouraged animal researchers to make projective suppositions about human anger.

But we are not simply another higher mammal. We are as different from the lower animals as God, if He exists, is different from us. We have evolved a massive cortex, the part of the brain from which all those special aspects of personhood evolve: all capacity to be imaginative, predictive, technological, verbal, poetic—and devious. Both the beast and the person may react with a violent unthinking rage when they view their young attacked, but the thinking person may delay his assault to serve his purpose. He may use cunning or guile, bide his time, plan his revenge, be duplicitous or hypocritical. In so doing, he must suppress the show of rage and ignore the physiological changes within him that are urging him to action which is less than self-serving. He has the capacity to ignore the crude emotional directives of a survival system he has inherited from his primitive ancestors. Nonetheless, he is stuck with their physiological and autonomic effects. He is left with a constant generation of this now useless stuff "anger," and it may consume him instead of his enemy.

The rules of the game of survival are entirely different for an organism like the human being who not only lives, for the most part, in a world of his own perception, but can also modify the true environment; who not only inherits a body and physiology but is capable of altering his own internal states, his own bodily functions and his own design. The problems inherent in this power to redesign ourselves and our environment emerged late in our evolution because our culture came late, and our recognition of these problems came even later.

First, of course, were the successes. We began to analyze those aspects of our existence which created misery, and we began to do something about them. But in order to treat sickness we had to understand its causes. With the discovery of the germ theory came the awareness that what we had previously defined as illness was in reality the body's attempt to repair the illness. The fever was not the problem; the chills and ague were not the problem; the pus was not the problem; the swelling, the heat, the inflammation were not the problem. These were the bodily mechanisms of protection, and while the abscess may have been that which was causing us the pain, it was in actuality protecting us against the true danger—the foreign body, or invader, at the site. Only after the great discoveries of the nineteenth century spearheaded by Louis Pasteur and Robert Koch did we begin to understand the nature of infectious disease and body protection. With that understanding came also the awareness that repair could go awry.

One of the more interesting aspects of misguided repair arises in the field of psychological illness. In the psychological area we always define health and sickness in terms of function. If a problem occurs and the solution works we generally call that healthy. Where the solution to the problem creates more havoc than the dysfunction we tend to call that illness. All psychological illness can be viewed as forms of misguided repair. If an individual has some vague dread or anxiety about his security generated from a multiplicity of unconscious causes of which he is unaware (it may be related to parental treatment in the past that left him feeling vulnerable; it may have arisen more specifically out of failures in competition with siblings; whatever the causes), and if the person's rage or anxiety drives him to success, hard work, the stabilizing of his life, we will see this as a normal adjustment and consider the behavior "normal." "Normal," then, is always value-laden. In our culture it is heavily tied to the standards of pleasure and performance.

If in trying to control rage or anxiety a person displaces his emotions from his behavior to his body he becomes a hypochondriac. This does a good deal to control the anxiety. All a person now need do to relieve the stress is see a doctor. Instead of feeling inadequate and reduced, and unwilling to compete where he anticipates failure and humiliation, he discovers the medical solution.

The sick role is a nonculpable one. It garners sympathy (at least at first) rather than contempt. It also is a convenient device for punishing other family figures. An invalid can shirk responsibilities and tyrannize a household. Hypochondria also contains within its structure an alternative homeostatic device. To limit stress, avoid —now with medical approval—stressful situations. If stress breaks out, see a physician for absolute temporary reassurance about the anxiety, thus eliminating it. Rage instead at the fates, for the fault, dear invalid, is not within yourself, but in the stars.

At the same time, the average person, recognizing this as a "phobic" and therefore irrational response, will be embarrassed and reject it. Some phobics will accommodate at this level. For them it is a minor payment for relief from stress. If the sources of anxiety are large enough and continue to be generated, the phobia will have to extend beyond its original focus.

Some people do live well with limited neuroses. They learn to rationalize to avoid stigmatization; they can cite the number of people who died by neglecting their health in any specific year. They may, fundamentally, know that that is not the reason for their avoidance of competitive stress even while not knowing the true reasons. Nonetheless, avoidance and displacement often work.

One of the most ingenious, though least adaptive, solutions to terror, fear and rage is the formation of a psychotic delusion. Delusions are destructive, since they demand a suspension of reality testing. While the price that is paid for this suspension is excessive and makes life ultimately unlivable in a normal social atmosphere, the delusion originally serves an adaptive function. Consider the following example. A man has carried out of childhood an irrational rage against women, which is only intermittently controllable and which finally is seen as uncontrollable. He may then "protect himself" by projecting that rage onto his wife, now perceiving *her* as angry with *him*. If her demeanor does not justify this projection, he may suspend rational judgment and devise a scenario whereby anything his wife will do will be viewed with jaundiced eyes. Her

understanding affection will even be interpreted as seductive du-
plicity, an attempt to disarm him. He may build a delusion in
which, for example, he assumes his wife is trying to poison him.

By doing this, by elaborating the delusional fantasy, he has
universalized his experience, thereby making it less onerous to himself. It is reasonable and rational to be frightened and in constant
fury if someone is trying to take your life. By rationalizing the
experience he no longer need feel crazy or different; he has returned
to operating under normal and appropriate standards. And, finally,
he has found a mechanism that controls and limits the anxiety and
justifies the rage. As long as he does not eat at home, or does so
with great care and caution, he need not feel under attack. By
focusing the danger into one area of life rather than allowing it to
spill over and contaminate all areas he has found a limiting device
which permits him to operate. He is also then free to seethe with
justifiable anger.

These are "repairs" that are worse than the illness. They are
manifestly so in this condition because the stressful situation, the
danger to survival, is tragically and ironically only an imagined
one.

In the physical sphere similar kinds of misguided repairs occur.
Allergic responses are often protective mechanisms gone crazy. The
individual suffers not from the invasive pollen or mold but from
the anaphylactic reaction—an excessive, irrational defense that can
kill you—raised against a specific antigen which can only harm
him. Some of the antigens are, of course, toxic, but ironically, as
in the psychological examples, many are not.

Out of the pioneering work of Cannon, Hans Selye and others
we began to understand a great deal more about the nature of stress,
homeostatis, constancy and the roles these play in disease formation. There is no question that anger, with its powerful capacity to
initiate internal changes, is a dominant force in the stress reaction.
"Consumed with anger" we can indeed become. And while the
promise of early psychosomatics was washed away by the silly metaphoric and simplistic explanations that were offered (peptic ulcer
was once described as the bite of the introjected mother), the logic
and rationality of the etiological role of rage and anger in many

diseases remains. A more specific understanding awaits more sophisticated knowledge of human physiology.

In a sense all diseases are psychosomatic. It is foolish to fall into mind/brain dualities. Psychiatrists are asked these days if they are worried that the new drug research will put them "out of business." One would hope that every physician's aim would always be to be put "out of business." Beyond that it is a naive question. Drug and psyche, chemical and emotion are simply alternative windows through which we view the same phenomena. Franz Alexander, the pioneer in psychosomatic medicine, once stated that he anticipated the time in which the science of sound would be such that we could reduce a piece of music to its harmonics, counterpoints, frequencies, vibrations, overtones, modulations and the like with absolute perfection. The question will still remain as to whether we can understand the *"Archduke" Trio* better through such analysis or merely by listening to it. One must not see these as antagonistic mechanisms. A portrait is not an X-ray, yet each helps in its way in describing a person and making him understandable to an observer. One, of course, will be preferred in the hospital, the other over the living-room mantelpiece. Neither is a better view, nor a truer, more "scientific" or more accurate view.

It was the same Franz Alexander who said, "theoretically every disease is psychosomatic, since emotional factors influence all body processes through nervous and humoral pathways."[24] Among the disorders commonly considered psychosomatic are duodenal ulcer, hives, eczema, asthma, glaucoma, ulcerative colitis, myocardial infarction and hypertension. Current productive research is ongoing in these areas, as well as in the role of tension in headaches, obesity, rheumatoid arthritis, thyroid disorders, irritable-bowel syndrome of all sorts and even cancer.

Whether anger can be isolated and pinpointed as the specific arousal agent in certain conditions, as distinguished from fear and guilt in others, is, as I have said, a debatable point. What is not debatable is that an amalgam of powerful emotions in which anger is a central force is a major contributing factor in precipitating or aggravating these psychosomatic disorders. Repressed anger can do damage.

This has been manifest from the first brilliant early studies of Wolf and Wolff.[25] Because of an old shotgun injury in the abdomen of their lab worker Tom, they had access to a direct view of his gastric mucosa. Poor Tom has contributed more than his share of grief to the annals of medicine. By manipulating his emotions the researchers could study what happened to Tom's gut during moments of anger. With anger and its concomitant resentment they saw increased gastric motility, increased gastric secretion, increased blood engorgement. All factors that contribute to ulceration of the gastric mucosa.

This became only one in a long list of researches indicating the profound effect of anger on the gut. It must constantly be remembered that these gastric responses are not chance events; this activity of the bowel is a response to a threatening situation which at one time had to be either destroyed or escaped from. They are part of a survival pattern formed in a past that no longer has relevance.

Recent work[26] has focused on psychosomatic aspects of hypertension. High blood pressure is thought to be a major risk factor in cardiovascular, renovascular and cerebrovascular diseases. These disorders alone account for 55 percent of the total annual deaths in the United States. Sterling and Eyer in an intriguing study reviewed the data on essential hypertension. "They fit remarkably well the picture of chronic arousal. It appears that essential hypertension can be understood as part of a broad physiological pattern set by the brain."[27]

After reviewing the evidence that these high-risk-, high-stress-, high-anger- and high-fear-producing mechanisms delineate hypertensives in general (as evidenced by a greater incidence in high-tech societies over primitive societies, men over women, stressful occupations and the like), they conclude that "hypertension is part of the acute arousal response. When arousal is chronic the body adapts to the prolonged pressure elevation even when the primary stimulus for it slackens."[28] Remember, the stress may be real or the stress may be imagined. The reality that operates on our physiology is the perceived reality, not a measure of the actual world.

We are, then, stuck with the fact that the homeostatic function of the body may adjust to a "constant" emergency level even when that level is clearly dangerous. There has been adequate corroborating evidence from animal studies indicating how chronic stress alters body chemistry. Catecholamine metabolism on the cellular level is affected. This drug alerts for attack. And unfortunately, the increased level of enzyme in the tissues, with the increased sympathetic activity it causes, persists long after the stress has ended.[29]

It has been shown that the blood pressure of American children begins to rise sharply when they enter the competitive world of the educational system.[30] David Hamburg and his group speculate that "early experience might affect biological systems such that the organism's response is modified for a long time, or even permanently."[31]

It is from such data that the idea of the killing aspect of suppressed rage and anger has emerged. Recalling that catabolic arousal is maintained as long as the organism continues to *subjectively* experience the stressful stimuli, and noting that anger cannot always be expressed in ways that are both socially acceptable and physiologically satisfying, it would seem to follow that *suppressed anger* or anger inadequately expressed would be particularly maladaptive. This was precisely the conclusion a major research group reached. ". . . Strong support [exists for the] hypothesis that suppressed anger . . . is, in fact, an ideological component to elevated blood pressure, both systolic and diastolic, and consequently to essential hypertension."[32] The study on hypertension is paradigmatic. There are other studies which show the logic that links suppressed anger with diabetes[33] and many other diseases including cancer. The psychoanalysts have pulled away from their involvement in psychosomatic medicine just as the physiologists are beginning to find promise in it.

This damaging effect of repressed anger has been the basis for much of the rationalization for the therapeutic outpouring of rage. Well, the sad news is now at hand. Recent studies (R. Shekelle *et al.*; R. B. Williams *et al.*) indicate that *expressed* anger is hazardous to your health. Men with high hostility ratings have six times as much probability of having a heart attack. In addition, high hostility is associated with the risk of death from all causes. Expression or repression is not the issue. The problem is with the emotion.[34]

Those who deal with the psychological nature of human beings understand the power of the fundamental emotion of rage; and all who deal with the real social world are aware of how useless the mechanisms that produce anger are for coping with most current threatening situations. We no longer live in the jungle. We cannot pick up a club to destroy our boss—much as we would like to. In the long run we would more severely endanger our food supply that way than by swallowing our anger, groveling, smiling and submitting to his indignities. The incessant exposure to frustration, humiliation and reminders of impotence is the stuff of modern life and, so it seems, death. Anger is an important and appropriate response to many life experiences, but the physiology of anger prepares us for solutions that are obsolete. We do not protect ourselves, our security, our family, our home by direct attack. More likely than not, attack would endanger all of these. So, then, what has happened to that physiology we have outgrown? We may silence the voice of anger, but it will be heard; it will be felt; it may, indeed, consume us.

The problem is not in the release of anger. It is in the unwarranted generation of anger. The problem arises from the ability and the felt need to manufacture quantities of anger in response to ambiguous stimuli in the environment which are perceived as threatening our dignity and pride. This capacity to manufacture almost unlimited supplies of anger makes ludicrous all therapies that attempt cures for one's misery by making one angry. Even if one accepts the concept that fevers are bad and can be reduced by alcohol rubs and aspirin, this hardly suggests that there is something therapeutic in generating a fever in the first place just to permit the administration of the alcohol rub or the aspirin.

The problem with people who have pent-up emotions is usually not their inability to express them but their capacity to generate them. They do not need a weekend marathon of provocation and humiliation to express the very emotions which they generate to excess *without* provocation. No, I am afraid we are left with a much more complicated problem. In order to understand how to handle anger we must learn also how to handle a physiology that is discordant with the psychosocial reality we have created.

We are less rational than we would like to think we are. Much of our behavior is dictated by forces within us which operate—often inappropriately—beyond our reasonable control and even knowledge. We are more often threatened by symbols than by circumstances. We are knights devoid of quest, faith, illusion and romance. All that is left is the battle against enemies more often perceived than real.

Yet we cope. On our own, without benefit of knowledge or psychology training, we cope, as we have always coped. We find means to abide with anger. We "handle" our anger in such ways as come easily to our particular character structure and are within the limits of acceptability of our culture. In this way anger, if no longer useful, at least need not imperil us.

6. Handling Anger On Our Own

What, then, are we to do with the excess anger that we seem to be generating? How are we to accommodate this anachronism of a biological mechanism gone bonkers? If the biological stress reactions of anger are still all programmed toward the physical destruction of a threatening agent in a time when the threatening agents cannot be handled by physical destruction, we are in a peculiar situation. We have created a cultural malfunction. In the same way that neuroses have been described as misguided repairs, the physiology of anger is no longer beneficial, but is generating a more dangerous set of conditions than those it is attempting to resolve.

A perfectly functioning physiological mechanism is now out of skew with the new realities of our culture. And our culture is such as to have impeded the slow but elegant Darwinian selection that would have generated an increasingly effective species. Our culture is no longer conducive to the death of the weakest and survival of the fittest. Even if we could reasonably expect another million years of survival, it is unlikely that Darwinian evolution could genetically modify our anger response. We will not wait for that time. We will do one of two things. Either we will destroy ourselves because of that excess and inappropriate anger, or we will psychologically, genetically or pharmacologically engineer out the maladaptive functions of anger to fit our biology to our culture.

How have we facilitated group living thus far? We have so far ignored the cultural factors that generate anger, instead working out mechanisms for regulating the excess anger we generate. Some are effective, but most are costly. Designed to enhance survival under the new rules, they often add increased and unexpected measures of stress. We control and modify anger by different devices: we will at times "deny" our anger; we will at other times lash out in inappropriate rage at safer objects; we will be passive, and convert our passivity into an act of aggression; we may use paranoid adjustments; we may discover bigotry; we may, finally, collapse into the bankruptcy of despair.

A healthy person has a large repertoire of defenses against his own anger. The narrower and more constricted the available defense mechanisms, the more rigid and brittle the response, the more vulnerable he will be. Many of us characterologically will have developed preferred mechanisms. For purposes of simplicity, I will present the prototypic methods of handling anger in a more extreme form than is generally encountered in real life. The hyperbole allows for a clearer image of the traditional mechanisms. Most of us will identify such behavior as familiar; we all at times use all. Some readers, in addition, will immediately recognize that category which defines their preferred mode of adaptation.

DENIAL

Denial is a potent and primitive psychological mechanism of defense which is always difficult for the nonprofessional person to visualize or even understand. It does not refer to incidents in which we deny to others our responsibility for unfortunate events. It is not related to our response to another; it is an intrapersonal phenomenon. It involves self-deception. It means literally denying access to consciousness of a feeling, perception or insight which somehow threatens us. We simply avoid the danger by refusing to grant it recognition. Denial is seen at its most dramatic in the face of physical symptoms. There are individuals so frightened of ill health and so conditioned to the mechanism of denial that they will not see (literally will not perceive) certain changes occurring in their bodies.

There are events in my training as a physician that I will never forget. The first life that I saved; the first death to which I contributed; the first overt sense of denial I encountered. A rather obese woman in her late fifties or early sixties appeared in the outpatient clinic because she had a lump in her breast. The "lump" was a mass the size of a large orange. I asked the woman why she had not come in sooner. The answer was that she had just noticed it. Despite persistent interrogation the woman insisted that the mass had only recently developed. In this woman's mind the lump had appeared within the preceding few weeks. There is no way that a dense tumor mass (as distinguished, for example, from a fluid cyst, or edema due to a bruise) could have developed so rapidly. We do not expect an individual necessarily to notice small nodules, but certainly somewhere along the line a clearly identifiable lump had become discernible by direct examination. It does not require sophisticated palpation. Where was this woman when the lump was the size of a lemon or even a walnut? Sometime before the tumor reached this massive size it had to be detectable, palpable and unavoidable. She had to have recognized it.

The fact is that she did not. This capacity to ignore the evidence of one's senses is called denial. Denial is closely related to extinction —another function that exists on the simpler level of experience. Extinction refers to the capacity of the body to block from cortical perception (that is, from conscious awareness) a wide variety of chronic stimuli that continually bombard us. As you are reading this book, literally dozens of intruding stimuli may be competing for your awareness. If they were allowed access to your consciousness, they would interfere with your concentration and destroy that focus which is essential for the perception of ideas. At this very moment you may be "extinguishing" a fusillade of potentially distracting stimuli. A radio may be playing in another room; street noises may be intruding from outside; a flickering light may be disturbing your vision, or the failing light of darkening day—all will remain unnoticed until "called" to attention.

In addition to such external stimuli are all those arising from the internal world of the surfaces of your body. To be aware of them constantly would be maddening. One is unaware of the binding of a sleeve painfully compressing the armpit; the pressure of the shoe across the surfaces of the foot; the sensation of the teeth and soft palate on the tongue, the salivation of the mouth, the itching of the mosquito bite. One is unaware of them until they are called to attention, whereupon one immediately feels them. How is this possible?

There is an actual mechanism of neural transmission designed to diminish the perception of a chronic, unchanging stimulus. If someone rests his hand on your shoulder while you are reading you may be startled by the pressure and sensation of that hand. If that hand is allowed to remain there unmoved, a gradual extinction of the sensation will occur. The pressure of the hand is unchanged, since the weight of that hand does not diminish from one moment to the next. Why, then, will we no longer feel that weight? We are physiologically attuned to differentials—that is, change—and we have a capacity for extinguishing sensations that are chronic. This permits concentration which otherwise would be impossible. One has only to think of the difference between an arm resting gently on our knee and a finger constantly and rhythmically tapping on that same knee to see the difference in attention-commanding stimuli. To discuss the process of extinction before a class of students is to convert a quiet, attentive class into a rustling, restless, fidgeting, coughing, swallowing, inattentive mass of self-conscious and miserably uncomfortable creatures. It is easy to appreciate the extraordinary value extinction has in concentrating energies and focusing attention.

A teenager absorbed in a book or television program is not lying when he says he didn't "hear" his mother calling him to dinner, even though she may have called him repeatedly and she may have shouted at full intensity. He did not hear because hearing does not involve only the stimulation of receptors of sound. It also demands cortical involvement. The sound receptors of the *unconscious* individual are unimpaired, but the unconscious individual does not hear. To be heard, sound must command the cortex.

Some people never "hear" the sound of their own anger. These people are anesthetized to the internal turmoils that constitute the rage response. The degree to which the response of anger can be said to even occur if it is not perceived is still debated, proof being difficult in dealing with concepts of the unconscious.

At one time prefrontal lobotomy was widely used as a means of reducing and controlling intractable pain. Patients who would shriek with the weight of a bedcloth on their foot would sleep peacefully after such surgery. When, however, they were questioned in detail as to whether they were experiencing pain, they would, surprisingly, answer "Yes." When asked how then they could now sleep, and why there were no moans or cries of pain, they would say that they still experienced the pain, but that the pain was no longer "painful." I have no conceptual idea of what that could mean, but I have observed the phenomenon and it exists. Obviously there is a significant distinction between feeling pain and experiencing pain.

Similarly a catatonic can be pricked with a needle and provoked in every imaginable way to jolt him out of his catatonia, yet he will remain rigid, immobile and unresponsive, without any expression or other evidence of sensation. After the catatonic stage has gone into remission the patient will describe in great detail all the events that occurred during this period of catatonia. He had some method of registering an experience without acknowledging, recognizing or "experiencing" it.

No one can say with any authority what actually happens with the denial of anger. Certainly there may be two distinct and different phenomena. With light denial one may repress the recognition of the feeling of anger while registering all the complex responses, physiological and otherwise. With a denial that is profound one may actually abort the responses. I am not at all sure that the latter is actually possible, short of psychosis. The former certainly exists. I have had patients who clearly demonstrated all the physiological, emotional and expressive aspects of anger while insisting that they were not angry. With persistent interrogation they might be driven to the point of using euphemisms—admitting that they might be annoyed, disappointed or hurt, while still denying that there was any relationship between those emotions and that which most of us call anger.

I am not now referring to those people who can feel anger but who, for a multitude of reasons, have difficulty expressing it. They belong to another category altogether. That group could be characterized by a patient who, angry with his physician but afraid to express it, will, instead, advertise his emotion by recounting the incredible amount of time and money he has invested in treatment and by commenting on the "peculiar fact" that he is in much worse shape now than when he began. This split between experiencing and revealing is not what is meant by denial. Denial does not mean that you hide your anger from the person who provoked it. Denial means that you hide your anger from yourself.

In this sense anger differs somewhat from fear. Fear is such a readily identifiable emotion that it is hard to dislocate or relabel. That which passes for denial is often an entirely different phenomenon. The courageous, foolhardy or reckless individual is often counterphobic; he is aware of his fear but more frightened of his fear than of the events which precipitated it. His courage is an attempt at mastery and refutation.

Chronic deniers of anger do, however, exist. I recall specifically one patient who experienced a vague gnawing feeling in his stomach whenever he was angry. His symptom was physiological, and I was concerned about an ulcer, which he never developed.

It may well be that the mechanism of this denial of anger resides in that fundamental alliance between fear and anger. Many of us are too frightened of our anger to express it. With those who use denial the fear of their own anger may be so overwhelming that they cannot even tolerate its recognition. This fear can arise through two quite distinct dynamic channels. First, it may be fear of retaliation, in which case the vulnerable person sees himself as an inevitable loser, inadequate to most competitions. If he expresses his anger, it will invoke a more profound and destructive anger on the part of the other person and he will surely be destroyed. This intimidated individual has learned some unforgettable lessons from a brutal past, occasionally involving a brutal parent. Convinced of his inadequacy in open combat and always visualizing anger at the level of physical destruction, he represses the recognition of his own anger in the interest of survival.

The second dynamic mechanism is often derived from a similar background. Here that which is most frightening is the destructive aspect of one's own anger. The murderous rage that one is sure is contained—but barely contained—in the recesses of his innermost self is the terrifying agent. This individual feels he must never acknowledge anger because to do so is to convert himself into a murderer. Richard Herron, who hammered his girlfriend's head until it "burst open like ripe watermelon," was a model boy whom no one had ever known to be angry. Neither his mother, his colleagues, his priest nor Richard himself could ever recall an incident of anger expressed or even—according to Richard—experienced.[1]

This example must not be used to confirm the assumption shared by many that if they ever "let go" of their anger there would be mayhem and running amok. For the most part, and for most people, there would not. Merely visualizing rage in this way is sufficient to inhibit its expression. The number of people who commit murder every night in their dreams is vastly disproportionate to the number who would ever under any circumstances commit such an act. Would that we had the predictive capacity to distinguish the two groups.

Denial is a primitive device for "controlling" an anger that—for whatever reasons—is too frightening to acknowledge.

CATHARSIS

When my daughters, then eight and seven, returned from a week's vacation with their grandmother, they casually announced at dinner: "Grandma's funny." We answered guardedly, "How do you mean funny?" The older one then informed us that their grandmother seemed to have "a thing about BMs."

This logical conclusion was drawn from the fact that their grandmother in her dutiful way questioned them each morning as to whether they had had bowel movements the previous day. Since bowel movements had ceased being a subject of conversation in our family past the age of toilet training, this was interpreted as a peculiar, fetishistic preoccupation on the part of their otherwise conventional grandmother. It took extensive discussion to convince my children that what they had experienced was neither so morbid nor so fascinating as they had hoped but was simply another example of generational difference. They could not know that when I was a child a hot-water bottle was always called an enema bag, since that was the primary use made of it in the household. While some attention is still paid in certain parts of the community to "regularity" (how else do we explain the radio commercials and continuing sales of laxatives?), there has been a marked diminution in concern with colonic activities.

These days a discussion of catharsis and cathartic effects is more likely to be in relation to expressions of anger. The amount of time spent by serious people in serious discussion in serious places (in print) about the value of regularly discharging anger and the danger of obstructed anger is really quite remarkable. I am not sure that we are yet at the point where a modern-day grandmother will ask of her grandchildren whether they got angry yesterday or not, but that may be only because the concern with catharsis seems to have been displaced upward (along with the organ of discharge) from the child to the adult.

This simpleminded and extraordinarily wrongheaded solution —to let it all hang out, as though the catharsis alone would solve the problem—has found particular favor at a time and in a subculture that have glorified the self and therefore self-expression. This cathartic solution ignores the fact that the public space is mine as well as yours and your desire to ventilate yourself is an intrusion on my desire for peace and quiet. People's inner feelings have no *a priori* claim to public recognition. Quite the contrary: the private life of the narcissist, like the private parts of the exhibitionist, ought not to be hung out—uninvited—in the public space. We have a responsibility not only to the social unit, which demands a certain amount of evasion, reserve and dissembling, but also to our personal dignity to keep "it" in. Besides, as we have seen, it rarely does much good.

The cathartic model is a peculiarly physical one for this age of biochemical physiology. The closest extant example is probably that of lancing a boil. A boil is an accretion of perfectly normal substances, pus, produced to prepare the body for a threatening invasion—in this case a foreign body—which is producing pain because of the increased pressure due to failure of discharge. The solution is to lance the boil, permitting the discharge and bringing almost instant relief. Repressed anger is also presumed to produce "pressure," and catharsis, relief. The analogy simply will not hold. The conditions that generate anger are neither that specific nor that simple. The mechanics of anger are complex and extended and certainly not initiated by some chance event, like a foreign body.

Besides, the problem is rarely with the inability to discharge anger but rather in the capacity to constantly generate an excess of anger. The characteristic modes of handling anger are built into the character structure of the individual. Simple catharsis, like simple anything, will not change character.

In an individual dominated by anxiety, the discharge of anger may do positive harm. The awareness of his own rage may be so terrifying as to undo any relief from stress he may have had. Similarly in a person whose dominant emotional mien is guilt, the release of anger may leave him sleepless with agonies of self-depre-cation at his cruelty, meanness and thoughtlessness. Peace of mind is never simply a matter of anger present minus anger spent. We are more complex than that. Our relations and our perceptions are intricate scenarios, balancing multiple needs through the delicate interplay of many emotions. Only an animal whose emotional life is uncomplicated by such feelings as guilt, pride, shame and vanity could achieve peace and tranquillity exclusively through the emergency emotions of fear and rage. Catharsis was a "discovered" solution foisted on a receptive population during a particularly narcissistic phase of our culture. This solution should now be retired along with Primal Screaming, Esalen, est and their ilk.

TAR BABIES: THE PASSIVE-AGGRESSIVE

One who is afraid of his own anger always has the option of never exposing or displaying it, but that is no easy task. To stem the tide of an emotion charged with the power necessary to preserve security will always be difficult by design; fail-safe devices are constructed to resist reversals of judgment. Emergency emotions are built to operate above and beyond the resistance of cognition. Most of us simply cannot go through life containing all our anger all the time.

One convenient device for expressing anger while preserving caution is to disguise the anger, to offer the assault in the form of something else. Sarcasm is a particularly depreciating way of being funny; it is at the same time a funny way of being depreciating. Sarcasm defies retaliation with the implication that to take umbrage is a sign of inadequacy, a lack of humor. "What's the matter— can't you take a joke?" By the time we have achieved maturity, most of us are well aware that jokes are very serious business. We make no apologies about taking jokes literally; they are meant to be taken literally. Sarcasm is an adolescent form of humor which most of us fortunately outgrow by the time we become adults. But the mocking, smarmy voice of sarcasm is still heard issuing at times from the lips of an adult, revealing the residual adolescent within. With sarcasm the intention is announced, although disguised as a game. I tell you I think you are a fool in terms that seem to suggest I am not serious.

Sarcasm may be seen as a borderline state between direct aggression and passive aggression. Sarcasm directly attacks but denies a hostile intent, hiding in the sanctuary of humor. Passive-aggressive behavior, however, is assault by indirection and disguise. The passive-aggressive, like Uncle Remus' tar baby, just stands there receiving the blows of his opponent, reducing him to frustration and impotence.

When we enter the world of the tar babies the aggression is never announced but is implicit in the results. These passive-aggressive individuals even deceive themselves into thinking that they harbor no aggressive feelings. They are amazed that they are so often misunderstood. They do not understand why everyone is always so angry with them. "What in the world did I do?" is emblazoned on their escutcheons. They are preeminently the whiners, the guilt vendors, the martyrs, the sighers and sufferers of the world— and the latecomers.

Chronic latecoming is a complex mechanism which serves multiple purposes. Some of my best friends are chronic latecomers, although they are not friends with whom I would go to dinner or the theater. Some latecomers deny their aggression, claiming simply to be chaotic people. If that were so, the pattern of lateness should indicate this chaos. They should be ten minutes late one time, a half-hour late another, two hours late a third time. If their latecoming is based solely on disorganization, then you have a right to expect that they be ten minutes early sometimes, one-half hour early another time and two hours early a third time. The counter-argument might be that it is the nature of chaos to exhaust time, to make the person less efficient and therefore always to bias the action toward the late end. I think this is a reasonably acceptable argument in isolated cases, although here I would still look for unconscious aggression. For example, is the latecoming invariable, or is it selectively directed toward vulnerable parties?

I do not trust selective latecoming any more than I trust selective violence. When a patient tells me he has no control over his violence as an apology and exculpation for his having beaten his wife, girlfriend or child, my logical next question is "When was the last time you physically attacked a policeman, an employer or a man younger and stronger than yourself?" Invariably these people with uncontrollable rages manage to control them in situations of danger to themselves. Similarly latecomers have their selective "on time" appointments.

Some latecomers, of course, are people so dominated by fear that latecoming is a device for postponing any event—which in their cases means all events—that presents a potential for testing or confrontation.

Typical latecomers demonstrate a characteristic pattern of lateness, the design often announcing the latent meaning of the act. By the time a patient of mine arrives ten minutes late for the fifth time in a row—with the full knowledge that we have a limited forty-five minutes to undertake what I consider very important business and what I hope he considers with equal seriousness—I feel obligated as a psychoanalyst to correct his "Sorry I am late." I notify him that he is not late. When he looks at me with bewilderment, I insist that it is as difficult to come precisely ten minutes late for every appointment as it is to come on time and that I presume he prefers a thirty-five-minute appointment to a forty-five-minute appointment and wonder why. I have at times offered to schedule a thirty-five-minute appointment. The offer has never been accepted.

Given the elliptical nature of the psychoanalytic process, I do not ask him why he is angry or frightened; whether he was trying to provoke me; has he some pleasure in keeping me waiting, was some purpose being served, was he playing out some scene of which I am unaware and of which he may not be cognizant. I simply ask him why he is late and refuse to accept his assumption that his lateness is, somehow or other, independent of his intentions and purposes. A patient will start by believing he has no control over this action and often will be ignorant of the mechanisms behind the latecoming. He will not be able to answer the question. A psychoanalyst does not, for the most part, ask questions to which he assumes the patient knows the answer. He asks questions to probe for unconscious motivation. The very fact that the patient does not know the answer will drive him to examine the behavior.

Unfortunately—or perhaps fortunately—we are not free to deal as directly with our friends in a world of social intercourse. As a result we do not address their latecoming as an assault on ourselves, our time and our worth. We would be considered boorish and prickly. We laugh it off. "Everyone knows" that Dick or Jane is always late. But everyone does *not* know so, and most people perceive being kept waiting as a form of mild humiliation. The latecomer gets paid back one way or another, whether he is aware of it or not.

Lateness, like most psychological symptoms, is an overdetermined phenomenon. Every symptom is the final pathway for a dozen different conflicts, and therefore has a dozen different meanings. Lateness may represent different things to different people at different times. But there are common ingredients. The latecomer ensures that he never has to wait for anybody by making sure that everyone will be awaiting his arrival. His lateness serves both to elevate his status and to narcissistically call attention to himself.

These status aspects can be further advertised by special qualities of the lateness. I have an acquaintance, an erstwhile friend, whom I now think of as "The Admiral." It was only after she was a houseguest that I appreciated the quality of her lateness. She managed to convert my role from that of a companion to that of a hireling. When we went on an outing she was always the first to leave the car. When she appeared at the beginning of the day, invariably a few minutes late, she would patiently wait outside the car until everyone else had entered, opened the windows and cooled the car, and then, quietly and graciously—in her most ladylike manner—she entered the vehicle.

Her action was so studied that my wife decided to test her limits by outwaiting her, and a small drama of manners was played out. It was the stuff of which farce is made: the two of them devising elaborate excuses to delay the moment of entry—my wife as part of a testing ploy, The Admiral as part of a routine way of life. It was the amateur against the pro. My wife never had a chance. It then occurred to me that what was being enacted was precisely the privilege of rank in the Navy. The ranking officer was always the last to enter the boat (small craft) and was always the first to leave. We all waited for him and followed after him. This minimized his discomfort and announced to all bystanders, interested or otherwise, the exalted nature of his rank.

Latecoming is a typical example of passive-aggressive action. The multiple ways in which anger can be expressed through passivity are varied and wondrous to observe. The term "passive-aggressive" is something of a euphemism. Not all passive-aggressive behavior is passive. Two distinct elements are universally present: the aggression is always couched in behavior that can easily be rationalized as nonaggressive (even presented as a service), and there is a vague and indirect quality to this form of aggression that resists frontal attack. One can affront someone's steely anger with a blow and he will respond in kind, but as with the clash of swords there is the risk that one might break. The passive tar baby will never run that risk. He has safer measures. He is a master at the craft of deflecting direct expressions of anger. You strike him and he will not strike back. The stickiness of his response is his ultimate defense, binding you in an intricate web of passivity. The tar baby will do anything but display anger. He will weep, be humble, be forgiving, be understanding, even be comforting, so that each blow inevitably traps you in a further embrace of impotence.

A favorite device of the tar babies is the generation of guilt. They are master martyrs, but to be truly effective they must be bound to their targets with lines of affection. During my residency I once treated a six-foot-four-inch Irish stevedore who broke up the ward in a violent rage following a meeting with his gentle, sweet, devoted mother. He ultimately explained the relationship. He had never seen his mother angry or anything but self-sacrificing. Growing up in the Midwest as one of five brothers, he would arise early on a cold morning only to find that his mother had anticipated him. She had shoveled the snow from the walk, trudged to the village, secured fresh rolls for her sons' breakfast. The power over her five sons of such service was overwhelming. They lived in a constant state of guilt. They could never repay that kind of devotion. A lifetime of service would never retire that debt. If they upped the ante she would up the ante. Eventually they were reduced to a state of impotence in the face of her martyrdom. Any overt display of anger would only serve to bind them further to this particular tar baby. Their anger would elicit only signs of forgiveness, love and devotion. To be angry with your mother because she gets up in the morning, shovels the snow and gets you hot rolls for breakfast is to be an ungenerous beast. To express that anger and have it received with kindness, love and apologies instead of retaliation is enough to reduce even a six-foot-four-inch stevedore to tears—and a rage of violence on a hospital ward.

The tar babies' repertoire of passive-aggressive behavior is limited only by the bounds of human ingenuity. They can be accident-prone and manage to damage your most precious possessions. The accident-prone are a large, heterogeneous population. While some accident-prone individuals are self-destructive, insecure and anxious rather than angry people, there are those who always manage to spill on others rather than on themselves. We have a right to be suspicious of this population.

The tar baby always absolves himself of responsibility and guilt. His repertoire often involves the manipulation of guilt, either directly or indirectly. If he occasionally chooses to open an encounter with an aggressive action, he is merely saving the guilt for the second round of the battle. When we counter his initial thrust with a reciprocal anger, he will parry with understanding, or better yet, hurt, pain, tears and grief, all obfuscated by a miasma of perplexity as to why anyone as well-meaning as he should have been so badly used. One always loses the second round to the tar baby because he is a master of confusion and an artful dodger. The tar baby's signal of anger is never as explicit as a slap in the face or a boorish statement. Confusion is part of the tar baby's assault. His techniques obscure reality, raising questions as to what actually took place. Perhaps we were wrong, perhaps we misunderstood him, perhaps we even projected our own anger. Our doubt becomes the opening for the introduction of his passive attack. The tar baby is an "infighter" who will embrace us to pummel our conscience with small and painful jabs.

In defense of passive aggression, we must remember that it is most common in a person who, for multiple reasons, is incapable of utilizing more direct, and often more brutal, expressions of anger. It is common with the adolescent. His one defense against the power and authority of the parent may be sloppiness, lateness, refusal to eat or any self-destructive behavior that exploits the love and solicitude of the parent in the service of retaliation. Passive-aggressive behavior is often closely associated with women who, frustrated and frightened by their inability to physically overpower a more brutish man, must find some means of equalizing the physical disparity.

An interesting subgroup in which strong passive-aggressive features appear are those men who suffered the loss of a mother during their adolescence. In the normal relationship of a young boy to his mother the show of affection will be in one direction only. The son may experience feelings of love but he very rarely articulates or overtly expresses them. In our mean-spirited culture that bars women from experiencing achievement and men from loving, it is only with the confidence of maturity that men can feel free or safe enough to tell their parents of their affection, and for some, tragically, not even then. When a parent, particularly a mother, dies during the child's formative years, he is left with an overwhelming sense of guilt toward this woman and often will displace that guilt onto women in general. He will shoulder that burden of guilt his entire life. Having received more than he has given to women (as symbolized by one woman, the mother), he will atone through a marked generosity, forgiveness and a reluctance to express his anger directly. But he will feel anger, often excessively, since he also has been "abandoned" by a woman during a crucial period of need. His only apparent defense may be a passive-aggressive adaptation.

While the repertoire of the tar baby is exhaustive, its salient features are fairly constant. Aggression, while present, is always masked. Even when he evokes anger he will not respond in kind. Finally, he binds the victim to him with sticky ties of impotence and frustration, guilt and shame.

GRIEVANCE COLLECTING

Some of us are sentenced by our own psychology to go through life in a constant state of deprivation. This feeling is independent of true privation and will exist in such individuals unabated by factors of reality—constant through poverty and affluence. Since deprivation, like privilege, is always cast in relative terms, there is usually someone available for comparison to one's own disadvantage. These individuals, on the border of paranoia, are distrustful and provocative, convinced that they are always taken advantage of and given less than their fair share. They are often right. There is something about the defensive attitude of a paranoiac that invites just such behavior. The irony is that after a while they begin to enjoy their own deprivation, to the degree that people with this kind of adjustment can be said to enjoy anything. They are unhappy with the burdens of success. Deprivation, particularly when it can be precipitated, not only confirms their most profound suspicions, it confounds their critics. They have been accused of being "paranoid"—overly suspicious, overly cynical, mistrusting. Each event in which advantage has been taken of them becomes a triumph for their bias. They are the beachcombers of misery, who see each grievance as a treasure to add to their collection.

Basic to the grievance collector is a constant comparative and competitive view of life. Everything is part of a zero-sum game. Deprivation can be felt in another person's abundance or good fortune. Somehow or other it is essential for the maintenance of the grievance collectors' view of life not only to feel deprived but to see instances of their own deprivation in other people's good fortune. Envy is the accompaniment of their chronic state of anger. It supports and encourages it. Why should they not be angry all the time? All the evidence they have collected confirms that they are unfairly and inequitably served at every turn. Somehow they have constructed a world in which there is only one winner—never they —so all winning diminishes them.

But it is not exclusively deprivation of material goods to which they are sensitive. They are also sensitive to slights and abuse. They are not simply deprived of the stuff and services to which others have access; they also are constantly being diminished. They are deprived of love and respect. Since they see themselves in a pervasive power struggle, they look everywhere for signs of their own humiliation. They are always given the worst table in the restaurant, the worst seats in the theater; it is their bad luck always to be in the longest line at the ticket counter, and their room never has the best view.

Like their more seriously impaired counterparts, true paranoiacs, grievance collectors are extraordinarily self-referential. They are ready to interpret all neutral acts as directed toward themselves. Group inconveniences are always focused and channeled through their own discomfort. Beyond seeing these events as happening only to them, they see them as happening because of them. It rains because they had planned a picnic that day. Even when there is no tangible person to blame, simply the rain from heaven, a metaphoric invisible agent will be manufactured. In their perception there is always purpose and intent, and the purpose and intent is to reduce them, to deprive them not just of goods but of respect and love.

Every analyst encounters a paranoid patient who will test the limits of his strength, self-control and professional discipline and eventually provoke him to anger. The sheer joy and pleasure the paranoiac realizes when the analyst finally succumbs is a wonder to behold. The ultimate confirmation of his view of himself as deprived and unloved occurs when even the professional (who is paid to take abuse and whose training is centrally focused on his controlling his own emotions, to maintain a nonjudgmental and neutral medical stand) finally succumbs to anger. To have broken through these powerful constraints is surely to prove that it is not only their imagination, that they are truly destined for deprivation.

One wonders why they do it. They have been compared to masochists who seem to enjoy their pain. Since I think most masochists do not enjoy pain, but rather endure their pain as a price they must pay for pleasure, I do not see this paranoid mechanism as a perverse anhedonic device. I think it represents something simpler: the acceptance of the emotionally impoverished world they assume they occupy. When you live on a potato farm in a time and place of poverty you damn well better like potatoes.

Grievance collectors are the children of emotional poverty. So bruised and damaged is their self-esteem, they no longer hope for love, luck or privilege. Deprivation is their due, and deprivation will be their lot. To hope for the good is to court disappointment and thereby compound their pain. To protect themselves from further hurt they anticipate the negative event. The pain is less when the event is expected. Instead of disappointment, they accept their bitter lot and find a nobility or dignity in enduring. They are joined with Tantalus and Prometheus, and the fact that they endure is a tribute to their courage and tragic nobility. They could spend their lives raging against such injustice and deprivation, but since there is little tolerance for outrage in our culture, they nurse their anger and embrace its causes.

In order to maintain this adaptation they must eschew genuine love, affection or generosity when it is offered to them. It is a pathetic adaptation. It protects against their rage at an enormous price in pleasure. They will never be hurt again. They will never be used again. They will never be humiliated again. So they will go through life with an armor that defends them against all gracious or gentle approaches. It is the price they pay to control their anger and to serve their equanimity.

A grievance collector must control a steady state of sullenness and anger with others who, by his lights, have taken all that is rightfully his. What happens to this anger? In part it is savored, as a confirmation establishing the rightness of his feeling of indignation. And partly it is handled by projection, a mechanism that is a central aspect of the more profound emotional state of paranoia.

Projection was one of the first mechanisms of defense to be described by Freud. It is the attribution to others of feelings that emerge within ourselves. These are invariably feelings of which we are ashamed or which for other reasons we find intolerable. By projection, a person with paranoid tendencies can dissipate some of the anger by assigning it to others. It is now *they* who are angry with *him.* Ironically, this same mechanism of projection contributed to the paranoid elements in his personality in the first place. Behind the sense that others are stealing his birthright lurks his desire to do that very thing to them. This is the projection of the impulse arising within himself to take by force that which was never given to him freely.

Why anyone adopts this mode of adjustment is difficult to say. A connection is often implicated between true deprivation and a loss in early sibling rivalry. There are children who are simply loved less than their siblings. It does not matter that the measure of love they get may be greater than that given to other children by less loving parents. It is the discrepancy that is painful. To see an extraordinarily successful thirty-five-year-old man bring into a psychiatrist's office a collection of pictures he has assembled from his childhood to "prove" that at Eastertime his basket was smaller than those of "all the others" and to examine these pictures carefully, courteously and microscopically and to honestly be unable to distinguish any essential differences is to be humbled by the power of early deprivation. I do not doubt that the patient who presented me with this carefully preserved "proof" of deprivation was in some fundamental and unremembered way treated differently and in that sense deprived. I know the evidence was not there in the Easter basket. This particular individual was a generous, warm and affec-

113

tionate person who had avoided a paranoid adjustment and was by no means a grievance collector. He had managed somehow to carry his sensitivity to injustice into the political sphere by becoming a social activist and a generous person with his time and talent. Why had he escaped? He had one of the basic elements for a sense of deprivation. Obviously, he did not have all. It suggests that all psychological and dynamic explanations are only partial answers, necessary but not sufficient cause. This lies at the heart of the "mystery" of why seemingly like environments do not produce like results in different individuals.

A grievance collector is not invariably a snarly and ugly person. He may have a cloud of misery always overhead, but he does not necessarily attack others with anger. Alternative mechanisms may dissipate much of the anger and allow him wary relationships with others, relatively free of strife. Generally, however, he will be patiently anticipating the disappointment and rejection which he assumes is the inevitable end of all his relationships.

BIGOTRY

In his brilliant essay on anti-Semitism, Jean-Paul Sartre says: "If the Jew did not exist, the anti-Semite would invent him." [2] In this statement Sartre summarizes the essential role of bigotry in our society. The despised object is not the cause of the bigot's pain but rather a part of the bigot's solution. The person with a predisposition to hatred must create an object for his hatred. An object on which he can project his frustrations, his anger and his impotence. Surely one felt this in the attitude of the cabby driving through Harlem. One need not minimize the broader purpose—the "pleasure" received—of that bigotry in the life of the cabby. The despised group is not just the object of anger, but the instrument for its relief.

"The hatred of the out-group serves the function of supporting the person who entertains it. However spurious the relief that comes from this type of defense, it is a vitally important function in the psychic economy of the insecure person. It is easier to reject others than to reject oneself. Yet what one rejects in others often reveals and intensifies what is wrong in one's self."[3]

Bigotry is yet another variation on the use of projection as a device for handling impotent rage. From grievance collection through bigotry to paranoia, the essential element is the use of projection as a device for dissipating anger and self-hatred. We cannot go through life distrusting and loathing the self on whom we are ultimately dependent and from whom we can never escape. We must find some means of denying the loathsome feelings within us. By projecting them onto others we make ourselves the subject of concern and pity rather than the mean and despicable creature we feel ourselves to be. We elevate ourselves at the expense of others. Projection accommodates well to the comparative and competitive view of the world entertained by those who use this mechanism. The projection of this internal set of feelings onto an entire generalized group, rather than onto an individual, is the essential component of prejudice.

Gordon Allport, in his extraordinary pioneering treatise on the nature of prejudice, states: "The net effect of prejudice . . . is to place the object of prejudice at some disadvantage not merited by his own misconduct."[4] Scapegoating allows us to find someone other than ourselves on whom to blame our misery. While it fences the other person out, thus seeming to protect us from the newly defined "enemy," it does more: "Fences are built primarily for the protection of what we cherish."[5] That which scapegoating protects is our damaged self-image and our fragile self-respect.

Prejudice is another example of the compulsion to assign guilt. We have carried the concept of individualism so far, we have aggrandized the self to such an extent, that individual responsibility is seen at the heart of almost every action. God has been dispensed with; chance is still not fully recognized, except in the precise and elegant world of physics and mathematics. Someone must be responsible for everything. By scapegoating we create not just one person but an entire class to whom all the miseries of the world can be ascribed. For self-protection we have a need to assign the guilt to some group of others, before some others can assign it to us. We create a despised minority.

We also protect ourselves from having to acknowledge all the anger that abides within us. To hate so much is to run the risk of identifying oneself as a hateful person. The bigot can assume that it is not his anger against them, but their anger against him that he senses everywhere. He can deny his own meanness which had been undermining his self-esteem. By projection he makes himself the compassionate victim and disavows responsibility for the angry, ugly world that surrounds him.

Behind all prejudice is passion. The passion of anger may be the only vital emotional energy left for the bigot. His passionate anger lends gratification to prejudice. It supplies the only "romance" in the mundane and unrewarding world of the bigot. He embraces his scapegoat, is obsessed with him, and the preoccupation, like that of love, gives him surcease from the arid and un-nourishing and passionless life he would otherwise be living.

Like the paranoid psychosis it so closely resembles, bigotry is a defense mechanism designed to rationalize and control that existential rage within from which there seems no escape. We are not irrationally and insanely angry, we are justifiably concerned. This frustrating and debilitating anger with our circumstance and ourself —neither of which can be controlled or altered—now finds a convenient means of solution. One can isolate and protect oneself— both positive steps—from the despised minority.

Scapegoating is a dangerous and destructive device for handling the rage, frustration and impotence generated by our society. It solves no problems. Even if it were morally acceptable it is rarely effective psychologically. We still carry within ourselves, only somewhat disguised at this point, a clinging anxiety about our capacities. In addition, the misery we impose on and disservice we do to the other innocent populations may ultimately impinge on our conscience. Somewhere at some time we may be forced to face the injustice of our acts and pay penance for our inhumanity.

Even if we are so heavily armored by rationalization that we can support an illusion of our superiority built by imposing inferiority on others, we do not escape without paying a price. The hated minority will dissociate themselves from us and the cultural values and institutions we represent. If we insist on seeing them as different creatures, as ants who are invading our picnic grounds, we ought not to be surprised if they then see us as different, as food to be consumed. We will be placed outside their realm of identity, and therefore outside their considerations of guilt and compassion.

The price paid by the despised group is another matter. These are the innocent victims of hatred, and they pay doubly. They are excluded from the benefits of full personhood in the moral community and they begin to assume their responsibility for that exclusion. They incorporate some of the hatred into their own self-image. They then must find a way of handling this diminished self-esteem. The anger it produces will be directed against those who have imposed on them this burden of self-hatred. They can then experience the justified rage of those who have been badly treated. The anger will be too extensive to be discharged only against that segment of the majority who have actively persecuted them. It will be dispersed into the general population from which the bigots have derived, thus making a bigot of the scapegoat himself. And again he will suffer. Often the awareness of the injustice he has endured will blunt self-assertion and ambition by providing a built-in rationalization for all his failure. His suffering will be compounded and his anger will grow.

DESPAIR

The relationship between anger and depression was first postulated more than seventy years ago by the pioneer psychoanalyst Karl Abraham.[6] From that time forward psychiatrists have empirically observed the peculiar reciprocity between anger and clinical depression. The evidence is overwhelming. The data accumulated from psychiatrists of varying disciplines and multiple theoretical persuasions confirm both the absence of rage responses in depressed patients and that the stimulation of anger, even artificially, has a salutary, if temporary, influence on a depressed patient. Closely related to this is the fact that excessive compassion, sympathy, pity or commiseration on the part of others will often drive a depressed patient to suicide. It tends to confirm his belief in the hopelessness of his condition. Within the profession, this has come to be known as "killing with kindness."

Because of the empiric data supporting a negative correlation between depression and anger, theories have been presented which proposed impounded rage as a cause of depression. The assumption was that an individual who for multiple reasons was unable to express his anger at a dead parent, for example, either contained it within himself, where it consumed him, or in a more sophisticated theory, deflected the anger backward from the dead parent to the self. This "retroflexed rage" was then seen as a key element of depression.[7]

It was a reasonable assumption. In depressions involving the death of a loved object, anger is often generated, and when it is, the anger is usually impounded. One of the responses to the death of a loved one is often a feeling of betrayal. "Why has he left me?" is the question posed in the unconscious. Such feelings of abandonment, confusion and pain are part of the irrationality that characterizes our attitudes toward death. More specifically, they may be an expression of our unwillingness to recognize the often unpredictable, seemingly random, and therefore ominously uncontrollable occurrence of death. Frightened by the prospect of our own death, we tend to deny its inevitability, and when the death of another occurs we tend to see it as a purposive assault. At first, particularly in accidental deaths, we may blame the dead with angry remonstrations that attempt to implicate the dead person in the responsibility for his own death. "If only he had not taken the car" is a classic accusation. To be angry with the dead is an unacceptable and unforgivable feeling. We tend to quickly repress that anger and convert it into the self-reproach and self-punishment that are so characteristic in depression. Over and over again, in dozens of reported cases, the recognition and expression of the rage has been a part of a successful process for therapeutic relief of depression.

The anger/depression linkage has recently been attacked on two fronts. One attack is founded on the accusation that psychiatric and psychoanalytic conclusions on the nature of depression are drawn from a biased sample, in that it consists only of sick patients. We are guilty as charged. That is roughly the equivalent of saying that surgeons draw conclusions about cancer only from sick patients.

Clinical depression *is* an illness, perhaps the most profound psychiatric illness short of schizophrenia. "Depression" as used in clinical medicine does not mean what the layman means when he says "I feel depressed." It bears little or no relationship to the concept of feeling down or feeling blue. Depression is a complicated set of mechanisms which constrict behavior, reduce the affect of the individual, destroy his coping capacity and almost delusionally distort his intellectual and rational functions. It is painful to a point of unbearability. When it is lifted patients discuss it as though awakening from a nightmare. They can still recognize the problems that precipitated their depression, still worry about their isolated and lonely state, their humiliations, frustration, impotence or economic peril—but it will be a different kind of worry. It will be real worry; it will not be depression. If conclusions about anger and depression have been drawn from the empiric body of medical evidence, that is as it should be.

The second criticism leveled against the anger/depression theory has stemmed from the recent development of antidepressive drugs. The naive critics assumed that the drugs were an alternative to exploration of the dynamic. These drugs have long been anticipated by the very psychiatrists who have used the anger theory to explain depression. The light-switch—all-or-none, on-or-off—aspects of depression have suggested a specific biochemical induction device. Notice that I say specific biochemical, not simply biochemical induction. All biologically trained physicians and psychologists assume that *all* body functions, motor and perceptive, have a final end point that involves the chemistry and physics of the body. What else would mediate these changes? Chemistry is not an alternative to psychodynamics, only an alternative language. There will always be phenomena that will be better understood by one language than by another. Seymour Kety once said, "There will no doubt someday be a biochemistry or biophysics of memory—but not memories."[8]

Those not trained in physiology must shake themselves loose from this mind–brain, emotion–chemical dichotomy. Think of energy as an analogy. It does not matter what stokes or powers the engine: coal, oil, gasoline, a man on a treadmill, sunlight or a waterfall. The stimulus is converted into a final form of energy which again may have multiple forms: heat, light, electricity, a moving piston, a rotating wheel. Current sophisticated studies of allergy (one could substitute hypertension, glucose metabolism or any number of complicated physiological events) demonstrate the synergistic effect of emotions and chemicals. Specific allergies can now be directly related to the action of specific antigens. The allergic response can be precipitated by the introduction under the skin of specific antigens, and only by those antigens. Other proteins will not produce the allergic response. Yet for years there has been a coexistent theory that allergy is related to emotional life. This was not sucked out of any psychiatrist's thumb. It was the product of equally careful empirical research. Neither set of data contradicts or precludes the validity of the other.

Years ago, during the time when it was assumed that the clean, clear air of the mountains would relieve the allergenic effects of the contaminants in city air a home for asthmatic children was established just outside Denver. One of the phenomena observed was that as soon as the asthmatic children from New York City crossed the river into Newark their symptoms seemed to diminish. The air of Newark is not appreciably better than the air of New York City. It soon became apparent that it was the separation from home, with its stresses, that was the therapeutic agent. Does this mean that the concept of protein-particle allergy is wrong? Of course it does not. There is a final common pathway for certain behavior, and multiple stimuli can initiate a series of events that ends by traversing this common final path, which in our example is the production of an allergic response. It is not theory but fact that tension can raise blood pressure. It is not theory but fact that we can alter in measurable ways specific chemicals and hormones in the blood of animals and human beings by conducting frustration experiments on them.

The emotion—chemistry dichotomy is destructive and must be put aside. We are entering a new era of biological understanding of behavior. Electrodes, surgery and drugs can already modify behavior. They do not, nor ever will, displace ideas and emotions as motivators.

The current debate over the etiological basis of depression anticipates future debates on rectification of social ills as well as personal pain. Much of the anomie of modern life may be viewed as a social equivalent of depression: lethargy, hopelessness, helplessness and despair are common to both. To discover the chemical end point that triggers a feeling in no way nullifies the relationship of that feeling to the social stresses which were originally viewed as its antecedents. Nonetheless, the critics of the anger/depression theory may have a point. To see a constant relationship between two sets of data, whether positive or negative, while always a significant piece of scientific evidence, does not establish a *causal* relationship. It may be that they are both products of some third agent; it may be that that which is seen as cause is really effect; or it may be that one is a necessary cause but not a sufficient one.

The evidence is not complete. Perhaps repressed anger does not cause depression. Perhaps it does not even contribute to it (although there I think the evidence is quite good). Nonetheless, the fixed relationship between the impounding of anger and the feeling of depression is an empiric fact that will not go away. The problem may have been in the insistence of psychoanalysis on this as a single causal explanation. Our knowledge of mental illness, while incomplete in most aspects, is sufficient to indicate that most of our "diseases" are in reality categories of related conditions.

The traditional model for all psychological disease is the concept of misguided repair. The disease is an attempt to solve a problem that does not work. What is so apparent in depression, as distinguished from other mental illnesses, is the relative absence of such reparative maneuvers. The depressed individual has apparently given up hope and abandoned his coping mechanisms. Stripped of self-confidence and self-esteem, he sees himself as neither capable of initiating actions necessary for his survival nor worthy of surviving. He is hopeless and helpless.

Anger and fear, the basic emotions elicited during times of stress, are the first line, and oldest mechanisms, for ensuring our survival. The absence of anger, therefore, may be not simply a factor in causing depression but also a product of that despair. The physician who stimulates his depressed patient to anger is doing a number of complicated maneuvers all at the same time. Any stimulation may rouse a depressed person from the somnolence of despair. When he is capable of initiating an anger response it may simply be a sign of success rather than the cause of it. In other words, the flickering of the light bulb did not restore the continuity of the electricity; it merely signaled the return. Depression demonstrates the fundamental role that anger and its expression plays in the general adaptation of the human being.

GENDER AND CULTURAL DIFFERENCES

Originally psychoanalysis allowed for only one acceptable causative agent of depression: the loss of a loved object. I have never been impressed with the exclusive definitions of psychiatry. My earliest research in psychiatry was prompted by my noticing a distinct, gender-related difference between men and women who committed suicide.[9] Almost invariably women committed suicide following the loss of a love object, whereas male suicide attempts were always in relation to the loss of a business or humiliation in the man's professional life. Classical analysis, desperately attempting to preserve its generalized theory, insisted that the business or status loss experienced by male suicides must be "symbolic" of lost love. Fine! But why then did they jump out the window when confronted by only the "symbol" and not the reality? And why did women respond only to the reality and not the "symbol"? The answer was that both income and love were symbols. The real loss was self-worth, and that was differently grounded in the two genders. What both of them were experiencing was the loss of their self-confidence and self-respect.

In a society that sees a man's worth in terms of his achievements and judges a woman's value in terms of her relationships, status and esteem derive from different areas. In the past, gender stereotyping had defined different roles for men and women. Self-esteem was evaluated in terms of one's fulfillment of his or her role. For a man his survival was dependent on his occupation, his work, his earnings. For a woman her survival was seen as dependent on her relationships. When a man lost his fortune he lost his pride, self-respect and, beyond that, confidence in his capacity to survive. His instruments for coping were put to question. He no longer trusted his capacity to make it in a competitive world, and he drifted into depression. Precisely the same thing happened with a woman who was rejected in love. She lost what she saw (even if this was a cultural artifact) as her essential coping mechanism—her capacity to attract a strong and powerful man to support her. The abandonment by a loved object placed in question her lovability and worth. The question of her survival became ambiguous in her own eyes.

The psychoanalytic model erred by expanding a specific case into a general truth. The traditional theory of depression was wrong. What we have with depression is a bankruptcy of self-confidence and self-esteem, from whatever source it may occur. With the erosion of gender stereotypes we should begin to see women becoming depressed because of the loss of a job and men entering depression because of rejection in love. What is evident is that there are different mechanisms for dealing with stress available to and compatible with the different roles assigned to men and women.

Implicit in so many of the examples and so much of the preceding discussion must be an awareness that there are gender differences in the handling of anger. Much has been made of gender difference in terms of response to frustration, men being more likely to respond with rage and aggression. Developmental studies on human beings clearly confirm what has been suspected from biological studies of animals. Androgens—male hormones—have been shown to promote aggression. The injection of female animals with androgens has made them adopt certain "male" aggressive stances. Injection of androgens into males makes them superaggressive. We are aware of the difference in circulation of androgens in men and women.

Developmental studies with children indicate marked gender differences in both the traits developed and the timetable. Boys are likely to be more bellicose and belligerent at every phase. Their motor skills develop earlier and their cognitive abilities lag behind girls'. Recent careful studies in social psychology[10] have pointed out the different roles that anger plays in the interrelationship between the sexes. During the course of playing, boys are constantly screaming, gesticulating, arguing, testing, threatening and fighting. To watch even so innocent and nonphysical a game as baseball is to expect violence to erupt at any moment. Occasionally it does. The important observation is that violence or no, the *game,* the activity, goes on. With girls it is different. When anger or confrontation emerges, the game is likely to be stopped. Here the event or the activity is obviously secondary to the relationship. The boys seem to risk the relationship for the primacy of the game. The girls will abort the game to protect the relationship. Gilligan and others who have worked in this field are careful not to draw conclusions about whether this is a product of acculturation or genes, although I sense a bias toward genes.

These gender differences in handling frustration are fascinating and extend beyond the games of childhood. One of the more dangerous games played by the average individual is not even articulated as such. This game begins when a typical man gets behind the wheel of an automobile. He is transformed. The automobile is an instrument of power. It is a distancing machine, and it is visualized almost in the way that the tank was in war. Protected by an armor of steel, with an increased capacity to safely flee if events turn against him, the average man can be reduced to a competitive, aggressive idiot. Name-calling that would never occur at the distance of three feet on a vis-à-vis basis takes place often from the safety of a car. Life-threatening behavior is a commonplace event on our highways. If someone cuts you off, endangering your life, while traveling at fifty or sixty miles an hour, the logical action would be to keep your distance from him. But a man rarely responds that way. He interprets the aggression as an attempt at humiliation, as a personal assault and, further, as a challenge that must be met. If his life was endangered, he will get even by racing ahead and cutting the other fellow off, thus endangering his life a second time. Such behavior has not been empirically studied, but I think anecdotal and observational evidence seems to suggest that men are worse than women in this area.

Women seem to prefer another kind of aggressive behavior in automobiles. I believe that women more often than men will hug the passing lane and refuse to move when "requested" by either a flashing light or a tap of the horn. I originally assumed that this was an anxiety about being in the middle lanes on fast-moving highways where cars might pass on both sides. Recently, I have been questioning men and women about driving attitudes, and now I am not quite so sure about my earlier speculation and tentatively offer another. Within a short period of time, a number of women, independently of one another, offered the same explanation. Yes, they hug the passing lane because they feel more comfortable in it, but they refused to budge because "I travel at the legal speed limit. No one has to go any faster than that. If they want to break the law, let them just go around me." No man I queried offered this defense. There is something self-righteous about this behavior, but in addition, it is characteristically passive-aggressive rather than directly aggressive.

Women are more likely to assume passive-aggressive attitudes in general because of the limited effectiveness of direct aggression imposed by body size. This may have biological roots. Certainly in prehistoric, pretechnological times it would have been disastrous to vest women's survival in anger-initiated direct assault. The physical disparity would have led to the destruction of the gender, and of course ultimately the species. Evaluation and adaptation demanded a differing set of primary responses to anger. When culture developed, it could have freed us from these biological differences, but until recently, it tended to reinforce them. Current developments have led to a quite opposite hope. The angry, aggressive masculine response that served so well in the jungle may now be making a jungle out of once civilized institutions of business and politics. At one time there had been hope that as positions of power and authority were opened to women, gender differences would alter the aggressiveness of men in business and life.

As barriers continue to fall that may eventually occur, but the early evidence is not so reassuring. One no longer hears talk that as women enter the boardroom and join the partners' conference table a less pugnacious, gentler, more negotiable, relationship-oriented atmosphere will emerge. In fact, those women who have achieved such positions are generally indistinguishable in behavior from the men. One does not sense any special "feminine sensitivity" or "lack of belligerence" in a woman district attorney or Supreme Court justice. This simply points out how flexible are human beings, how ready we are to modify even biological directives in the service of cultural concerns.

Part of the problem lies also in the nature of statistics. To say that women are generally more this or generally more that tells one very little about any individual woman or man. It is the nature of statistics to speak of groups. In the danger of generalization one may forget that the deviation from the norm within the group allows no predictability about the characteristic behavior of *a* man or *a* woman. The elimination of gender stereotyping will solve many problems and reallocate others, but is unlikely to alter much the amount of aggression generated by the frustrations that have evolved in the industrial society.

While recent work has demonstrated the ways in which the expression of anger is modified by the two sexes, most writers in past years have carefully avoided theorizing as to whether the scenarios acted out are culturally determined or biologically based. They are simply observations. We should not be afraid of making either deduction if we feel it is true.

If there is a second message paramount in my discussion it is that we are not the slaves of our biological nature. If it is true (as the evidence indicates) that androgens influence aggression disproportionately, well, then, so what? Aggression is not achievement; aggression is not even assertion; and even if it were, we are always free to ignore biology.

Every discussion of gender should start with consideration of biological differences and end by dismissing them. We are capable of changing our nature, and we are encouraged to by the very nature that created us. We sacrificed the security of Eden for the freedom that is the human enterprise. That freedom encompasses the capacity to do bad as well as good; to modify ourselves as well as our environment. We were "meant to" have dental cavities and we were "meant to" chlorinate our water so that we will not have cavities. The same God that created you and me created the measles, polio and smallpox viruses and we have eradicated them all; even the most committed environmentalists have created no fuss about endangering these species. We were given no wings and we fly. We were given no gills and we go underwater. We were given a Mendelian set of genes which would naturally require each generation to rediscover fire and the wheel, but we operate under Lamarckian principles. By developing language we have discovered a means of transmitting knowledge and the acquired characteristics of culture across generations.

We need not be afraid of biological differences, particularly when we feel they are destructive to the social order and create an inequity in the nature of things as we want them. We are perfectly free to change the biological emphasis. Remember, our biology is not an imperative or a command, as it is with other creatures, but only a suggestion. If we decide that justice and fairness demand different roles for men and women it makes little difference whether we were "meant to be" male hunters and female home and child carers. We were also "meant to be" the authors of our own future.

"Neither a fixed abode nor a form that is thine alone nor any function peculiar to thyself have We given thee, Adam, to the end that according to thy longing and according to thy judgment thou mayest have and possess what abode, what form, and what functions thou thyself shalt desire. The nature of all other beings is limited and constrained within the bounds of laws prescribed by Us. Thou, constrained by no limits, in accordance with thine own free will, in whose hand We have placed thee, shalt ordain for thyself the limits of thy nature . . ."[11]

What I have described are the predominant modes and mechanisms of dealing with anger in the American culture of our time. I acknowledge the distinctions between cultures, as I would acknowledge that the lessons learned here can be applied to other cultures only through modifications. Nonetheless, the different devices utilized in different cultures are all derivatives of the same biology. An understanding of the relationship between the biological urge of rage and the methods for handling it in societies in which brute force no longer guarantees anything, except possibly a few days in a jail, is constant and the same across cultures.

The devices we, as individuals, have evolved to dissipate and control a maladaptive anger are ingenious. These anger-controlling mechanisms are shaped by our culture and its values, but they are also influences defining our culture. We are, I believe, tolerating more brutality than is wise; we are legitimating more selfishness than is safe.

Modern psychology is floundering. It offers very few new messages, and fewer still are messages of cheer. Only very recently has it even begun to recognize the essential communal nature of our species. It focused too closely on internal struggles. It loved—not wisely but too well—the individual.

We must look beyond the individual, to the society. We have spent enough time and energy devising individual means of coping with anger. We know that culture can change in a relatively short time span. The formal behavior that was appropriate at the turn of the century seems archaic and distant to the grandchildren of the people who scrupulously observed it. We must begin to at least think about ways of redesigning our institutions. To start that process, we must examine that which generates rage in our society, so that we may devise methods of limitation and control.

7. Angry All the Time

To walk the streets of a typical American city is to see anger everywhere. To live the competitive life in an urban setting is to feel, as a friend once said, "angry all the time." No one, of course, is angry all the time, any more than we are frightened all the time. But the hyperbole is closing in on reality, and is fast becoming a description of, a metaphor for, the fast track in every city—a portent of what is to come in those areas which may still operate with gentler methods at slower paces. In the past forty years we have seen, I believe, a frightening diffusion of anxiety and anger spreading outward from our urban centers and slowly poisoning our general landscape.

In the previous chapter I listed some of the elements that tend to increase the feeling of insecurity, and therefore the level of anger, in our operative life. Since this level may be approaching a dangerous threshold, we must examine the cultural environment in order to locate the sources of stress. What in our current culture is so threatening; what is exacerbating our view of our world as a dangerous place; what is reducing our sense of confidence in ourselves in relation to our environment?

Two distant and different lines lead to the development of anger. Anything in our society, in our daily life or in the broader existential facts of life that makes the environment seem more threatening will invoke anger (and, of course, fear). Anything that diminishes our self-confidence and raises questions about our strength, value or worth—in other words, our capacity to cope—will also invoke the emergency emotions. The vital balance between the power of "them" and the power of "us" will determine the degree of fear, the degree of anger, the presence of both or neither.

DIRECT ATTACKS

It has been a central thesis of this book that what threatens us in modern life is rarely direct physical assault. Obviously physical violence does occur. It is not the central source of our current insecurities. We have seen more violent societies and more brutal cultures in the past. The most destructive aspects of brute behavior in our society reside in the implications of that violence.

There is no more direct threat to survival than the mugger, the brutal husband or the battering parent. They can kill. They directly announce their intention to hurt and maim us through their behavior. They are often in positions of physical superiority to us. They are the agents for which fear and anger as emergency emotions were originally designed. They are the vestigial beasts who stalk the jungles of modern civilization. Yet ironically, even in these primitive cases the mobilizing forces of fear and anger seem particularly ineffectual. Anger is often less effective than fear, and both may be less effective than appeals for help. A call to the police may be the best hope for the woman confronted by her drunken husband. In hand-to-hand combat she is inferior. She must secure the aid of the agencies of government that are designed and intended to protect the weaker from the stronger in a culture that has eschewed dominance by physical force.

An individual can augment his muscular system by his technological knowledge. He can substitute a gun for his biceps. A fragile woman is adequately protected from a powerful man if she has a shotgun in her hands and knows how to use it. This is not a solution that serves society well. The fact that so many of our citizens have

seen fit to arm themselves with everything from elegant purse-sized
.22s to bazookas and machine guns is testament to their fear and
rage, not to their logical analysis of how to handle violence in
everyday life.

Violence within the family seems more constricted, therefore
more controllable and to the community at large less frightening.
For the actual participants it is not. For the child it is certainly not.
For the woman who is economically dependent on the beast who
beats her there is a real question of her ability to alter the situation.
Nevertheless, intrafamily violence seems to have less capacity to
alarm the general public. It is unlikely to slosh over into the general
space. To an outsider it is less frightening than the gratuitous
violence of street crime because it is happening in someone else's
home. We need not enter there. Family violence is less frightening
to us because, as with gang wars, it seems confined to its own
constituency. The possibility of injury to innocent third parties is
remote. It is the random, gratuitous and ubiquitous character of
street crime that feeds our fear, anger and finally paranoia. Here
there are no control mechanisms. We can avoid dangerous places—
unless all public places become dangerous. Then we walk with fear.

To walk the city streets and to be mugged is a violation of the
sense of general order; it denies that we live in a lawful society. The
current preoccupation with law and order is a valid concern.
Granted, our concern transcends the actual amount of violence
occurring in the streets. We are not yet at a point where every
individual has experienced a mugging in New York City, but I
have yet to meet an individual who does not have a relative or an
acquaintance who to his personal knowledge has gone through this
experience. Pam McDonnell, a founder of the Safety and Fitness
Exchange in Manhattan, estimated that before age sixteen, 25 to
50 percent of New York City children will be accosted in some
way.[1] Such experiences are of crucial concern, for their direct as
well as their symbolic implications.

There is a prevailing feeling that the streets are meaner than
they once were. The sociologists attempt to reassure us with statistics that indicate one was more at risk in walking the streets of
London in 1884 than the streets of New York in 1984, and we are

not reassured. Our standard of comparison is not 1884 but 1944, and we *know* we were safer then. It is no more reassuring to talk about 1884 than it is to talk about the safety of leaving the cave in 20,000 B.C. We are right to reject the sophistry of such data. We know that we have regressed in the past generation, even while acknowledging the progress over centuries.

The statistics of street crime in the thirties and forties clearly indicate a lower level of violence than we have now. The thirties and forties were periods that whole generations of living people have experienced, and they sense the difference. When they say things have gotten uglier they are alluding to their life span, and in that time span things have.

Alan Stone, former president of the American Psychiatric Association, concerned about the growth of crime, reports that according to one well-known statistical study, in 1940 a citizen of Manhattan had one chance in ten of being a victim of a serious crime in the course of his lifetime. By 1970 the risk had grown to only a little better than one chance in ten of *not* being a victim.[2]

People in the middle class are particularly confused by sociological explanations and justifications for street violence. In part they have a right to be. Sociological justifications are often inexcusably simplistic. They are more likely to relate street crime to privation than to deprivation. The average man intuitively knows that they are wrong. After all, there was more privation in the 1930s than in the 1980s and yet there was a greater sense of community safety.

Anyhow, statistics are cold comfort. The fact that the majority of people who are intrepid enough to walk through deserted city streets at night escape unmugged is no incentive to play that game. When the percentage of muggings rises above a certain level (well below the 50-percent mark), rational people will refrain from walking there. People did not have to think that every bottle of Tylenol had been contaminated to keep away from Tylenol. Five bottles out of five million were enough to unsettle the population at large. Perhaps irrationally so. The Johnson & Johnson company was certainly made aware of how the contamination of a relatively insignificant number of bottles of Tylenol could produce a major dilution of confidence in a product.

When we return to the statistics of street crime and speak of percentages such as 2 percent, 5 percent or 10 percent, we enter an area of overwhelming statistical significance. If I know a toxin affects 2 percent of the available red jelly beans would I ever eat a red jelly bean again, particularly when the bowl also contains green, yellow, orange and black ones? If I am excessively devoted to red jelly beans I may bitterly resent the fact that we cannot better control the dyes that are used in their manufacture, but I still will not eat red jelly beans. It is a minor inconvenience. But the streets and parks of our cities are not jelly beans. We are obliged to use them. If we cannot, it may seriously cripple our way of life.

We of the establishment have neglected the very real importance and the symbolic significance of street safety. This neglect on the part of the intellectual community is close to criminal negligence. I understand the rationalization. "Crime in the streets" was once used as a euphemism for racist philosophies. In order to distance itself from such racism, the intellectual community shunned serious consideration of the problem and rationalized its neglect by attempting to minimize the problem. Also, the statistics of street violence have a racial aspect which makes it difficult and embarrassing to talk about. The data fall within the area of mischievous knowledge that can just as easily serve the purposes of the bigot and racist as those of the humanitarian. We are reluctant to get involved with these figures.

But the statistics are real, and in those statistics are included real, live people who demand that attention be paid to these problems. Street violence is a human problem, not a racial one. While we may be concerned about the high incidence of blacks among street criminals, we must recognize the equally high incidence of blacks among the victimized public. There is a serious injustice being ignored when a black woman who lives in the ghetto is afraid to do her shopping at night, is forced to spend a disproportionate amount of her income on cab fares because she is frightened of the subways, finds herself incarcerated in her own apartment because the very community areas—the parks, the avenues, the public squares—that were designed for her purposes and pleasures have been occupied by a hostile and uncivil force. There are sections of every major city where the police no longer patrol. They are the booby-trapped areas of our cities. They have been abandoned to the enemy.

Security is not everything. Safety is not all. Freedom demands risks, and a free society will always be riskier than a police state. That we have erred in the direction of autonomy is good—there are few of us who would want to change places with the typical Russian or Chinese—but we may well have stretched the limits of individualism too far by forgetting a crucial biological imperative. Each human individual operates in the network of humanity. He needs other people to survive and cannot exist apart from them. Press individualism too far at a cost to community and you will as effectively destroy the individual as if you had cut him off from his physical support systems.

We are at the limits of individualism. It has taken the man who lives in the streets rather than in the world of ideas to remind us of that. The calls for help from the poor and the ghetto dwellers are beginning once again to make "law and order" a decent and respectable term. We are finally beginning to retrieve this honorable concept from the clutches of the racists who had preempted it.

Beyond the direct consequences of such threats of violence, we suffer from the symbolic implications. To feel frightened in the streets is to feel humiliated and angry with those responsible for our fear. It is to feel betrayed and be angry with the authorities who have ceased to protect us—who are seen as being more concerned with the rights and welfare of the offender than with those of his victim. It is to revive the outrage of childhood when the misbehaving child commanded more care and attention, and by inference more love, than the quiet and obedient one. It is a provocation.

Unfortunately, we will also be angry with the population from which the attackers are drawn, even when this constitutes an unjust and falsely perceived generalization. If it is Irish Catholic extremists who continually injure us we will begin to hate all Irish Catholics; if it is Arab terrorists who bomb our buildings we will begin to hate all Arabs. If the muggings arise predominantly from minority groups in our cities we may become generally sullen and hostile toward all members of the groups. The resultant anger or hate occurs despite the fact that even a modicum of intelligent evaluation would indicate that the vast majority of the Irish Catholics, Arabs and other minorities are decent, law-abiding and gentle. The law-abiding blacks in the city are the principal victims of street violence. Added to that burden they must carry the weight and hostility of unjust suspicion and displaced anger.

We must not overestimate the amount of street violence that actually exists; but we also must not underestimate the leverage of such violence or the powerful impact it has on the social and political milieu. It tips the balance of trust to distrust, of security to danger, of congeniality to rage.

There are many sources of "direct assault" on our survival beyond the physical. One such (which unquestionably transcends physical force in importance) is an attack on our financial base. The modern world operates on an elaborate system of metaphor. It is often the symbol rather than the fact with which we are dealing. Money is one of the preeminent symbols. Those who sell their services for money are as often concerned with the meaning of the wealth as with its purchasing power. Although money does buy many things beyond material goods, a hundred-dollar bill in the literal sense is a piece of paper. Yet it, or a number of them, can corrupt a Congressman, seduce a sexual partner, purchase health, pleasure and even survival; it can buy space, security and that which passes for love. Obviously it is not a piece of paper which does all of this but the fact that the paper is a negotiable symbol translatable throughout the cultivated world for whatever one values—goods, services or status.

The person who destroys me financially, who takes my money, is the modern equivalent of the person who, in a previous age, extinguished my fire, raided my cave, contaminated my well, ravaged my food supply, burned my barn or stole my horse. They used to hang horse thieves. That seems incredible these days, but it did not to the frontiersman who knew that the survival of his family might depend on that horse. The greatest perceived threat to our sense of security (with the possible exception of an attack on our sexual pride) is an assault on our financial structure.

The rage at the thief who steals our purse is almost less—because what he takes is a finite quantity—than the rage at the office colleague who threatens our job. Threats to economic survival are perceived as life-and-death matters.

I recall an event from the days when I was still unknowledgeable in the ways of New York City. On the southwest corner of Madison Avenue between 95th and 96th streets was a small luncheonette named the "Soupburg." The border of fashionableness then extended only as far as 86th Street. I had little choice, and when I opened my office in this block it became my standard base for morning coffee and for lunch. The Soupburg served a minimal selection of food. Coffee, Danish pastry, soup and hamburgers pretty much exhausted its menu. It was a small place of perhaps twelve stools. Because the 96th Street area in those days was still a low-rent district, yet close to the fashionable 70s and 80s, it abounded in private schools. The luncheonette was operated by a man in his early fifties and his son. The man seemed tough, mean and, indeed, angry all the time. I was appalled by his behavior. I would see anger mounting as he watched two polite adolescents sitting on stools next to me lingering over coffee and lighting cigarettes. He would eventually explode, telling them, "Get the hell out"; "This is not a goddamn lounge"; "Can't you see that people are waiting?" I had not yet adjusted to the tempo and abrasiveness of New York, and I found myself disgusted and defensive in his presence.

After three months of eating every breakfast and every lunch in that Soupburg, I began to know that man and to appreciate the extraordinary amount of labor that went into his efforts, the minimal amount of each check (a hamburger may have been fifty cents in those days), and beyond that, I became aware of what time and space meant in New York. He had only two peak periods in which to make the bulk of his money, the morning breakfast hour and the lunch period. He had twelve seats, and only twelve seats. A check would rarely get above the two-dollar mark. His livelihood was dependent on rapid turnover. He did everything within his power to ensure that turnover. He was a model of efficiency. I used to delight in seeing him operate. A good short-order cook is an artist.

He is extraordinarily facile. He must handle rapid orders with accuracy and efficiency. Orders must be anticipated to promote that efficiency, but must not be overanticipated, so as to destroy the freshness of the burger and the reputation of the establishment.

He did his part, but it was not enough. As fast as he worked, if anyone chose to loiter twenty minutes over a hamburger that could be consumed in five minutes his business was doomed. Those polite but casual teenagers were robbing him of time and space. That seat must turn over every five to eight minutes for him to meet his bills. In New York City, people physically fight over time and space.

To know all is to forgive all in certain kinds of human relationships. The man's behavior never changed. My attitude toward him did. I began to like him, and feel compassion toward him. That did not surprise me. He was a man working hard to support his family in an honorable way. What surprised me was not my changing attitude toward him but my changing attitude toward "them." I began to see the students as "the enemy," and to my horror and chagrin I would find myself seething as I gulped my coffee and hamburger watching two of "them" chatting away while prospective customers were waiting for space or, worse, leaving to find other space. In identifying with this beleaguered worker, I felt his anxiety and adopted his anger.

To this day I am ambivalent about my life in New York. Whenever I evaluate the cost of city life, the price I pay for its pleasures, I do so not in terms of external danger, what someone might *do* to me, but rather in terms of what is *happening* to me, to my internal self. I have become less patient. I find myself somewhat brutalized and coarsened, less considerate of the needs of others, less polite. At one time I took the essential me out into the public space. Now there is another me, and I do not much like him. I see the change when I travel to distant, less corrupted places (becoming progressively fewer in number). The *politesse* that still is practiced in smaller and quieter places in our country does not charm me anymore, but irritates me. I am still at my big-city pace when the only waitress in a small-town diner is lingering to chat with the only other customer about his family. I do not see it as a civilized or gracious act but as an erosion of my time and safety. I have taken my timetable with me, and I must move fast to survive. How could she not see that she is endangering my schedule, which in a symbolic way is my life, by her insistence on discussing things unrelated to the efficient delivery of food?

In such a way we will all be enraged by those elements which have become symbolically equated with our survival. If money is survival, then time is money, and space is money, and so it goes. The connecting line extends from survival to things only indirectly involved. While the line may be attenuated and devious, in our own minds it is continuous and direct. The number of things that seem to endanger us is constantly expanding through symbolic elaborations, and therefore the number of perceived threats to our survival increases. They seem to exist everywhere in every corner and in every ambiguous action. We have learned to see danger everywhere. I know that it is fashionable to think of our age as the age of narcissism. Fashion has a way of being one generation behind. The sixties was the age of narcissism. By the time narcissism became a popular issue it had ceased to have a central relevance in the social order. We live in a paranoid time. If the dominant pathology of the moment is anything, it is not self-involvement, it is alienation and distrust.

INDIRECT THREATS TO SURVIVAL: REDUCED SOURCES OF PRIDE

Under this somewhat awkward heading I would include all those things which involve a diminution of or attack on our self-esteem by the withdrawal of approval and support.

We are at our most vulnerable in our relationships with those about us in the particular area of approval and disapproval. Much has been written about the weakened structure of the family. The numbers of illegitimate children, fatherless homes and single-parented households all indicate that an incomplete support structure is becoming the norm in our society. This could not be happening at a worse time. There is not much left except the family. At one time our support structures were more varied and abundant than now. Our identifications were multiple: with neighborhood, ethnic group, church, club, lodge, fraternity, union, extended family.

These were groups with which we were united for a common purpose. The church had always been a center for identification and support and generated, beyond a feeling of community and security, a sense of purpose. The tenets of organized religion promised a reward for following clearly prescribed rules that was an alternative to reward here on earth. A person took comfort in the fact that by being "a good Christian," he would be rewarded by the Lord with a better life in a better place. If there was only pain here, there would be joy in heaven. The sense of duty and order helped one through an adversity that was, after all, only temporal. The demise of religion as a powerful organizing force in life (as distinguished from simply a sociocultural identity and activity) places further burdens on those support structures which remain.

The fading of religion left a vacuum that was not filled by any alternative moral authority. The field of philosophy compounded the problem: it abandoned the area of moral philosophy during the very period when it was most needed. Ethics ceased to be a central concern, not just for the common man, but for the intellectual community. Most of us these days can take little comfort from fulfilling a moral mandate because there are so few left in life. "Whatever became of Sin?" Dr. Karl Menninger was driven to ask in his book of that title.

If we can no longer achieve security by being a good person through fulfillment of our moral duties—thereby enlisting God's protection and love—we must look to external supports and external reassurances for our security. The desperate need for approval or reassurance must now be directed to those around us. Thus the power of social criticism and social ostracism operating on this intense need for approval became a strong force for conformity in our society. But if we feel that regardless of what we do we will never be found acceptable because of factors beyond our command —race, gender or other unchangeable factors—a growing rage and resentment will be our defense against the feeling of diminution.

Another traditional source of self-esteem has been the pride of mastery, the satisfaction of a job well done. But this too has been eroded. The nature of work has changed to produce less pride, while the opportunities for failure have increased. It may be preferable to approach the latter (and more complicated) issue first. Here we suffer from a side effect of a valuable aspect of our society, its mobility. We do live in an upwardly mobile society. The fact that it is less so than the mythology promises does not alter the fact that it is more so than in nineteenth-century Europe, from which so many of our forebears came. This mobility paradoxically makes it possible, almost inevitable, for an individual to see himself as a failure rather than a success.

In the traditional rural and small-town society of Europe, a worker generally felt he could not leave the role or even the locality that was defined for him by the accident of his birth. He generally accepted his social class as he accepted his height. His station was neither to be questioned nor necessarily to be abjured. If born into a small town in France in the nineteenth century with a father who was a baker or a shoemaker or a carpenter he would follow in his father's specific trade, and most likely in the very same shop. His ambition was limited by the opportunities of the town and the access to professional tools and skills.

Constricting it certainly was. All that he could become was a carpenter. On the other hand, to be a success in life all he had to do *was* become a carpenter! In an upwardly mobile society, however, unlimited opportunities seem to be present. The carpenter's son is free to become a cabinetmaker, or even a manufacturer. He can move from the working class into the entrepreneurial. Therefore to feel successful means not succeeding, but surpassing the father. In the fixed society, a man would be complimented by being told, even at age fifty, that he was "almost as good" a carpenter as his father had been. In the upwardly mobile society, the father's position is not the desired end, but rather the point of departure. The father's role (if not the father) is *not* the symbol of success, but rather the paramount symbol of failure. "What do you want to do," a modern father will ask, "end up like me?" The father is an accomplice in projecting his own role as a model of failure rather than a model of success.

The normal competition with the father is now intensified by the expectations of both that he will be surpassed. This will often produce guilt in the child and anger in the parent—and is a potential drain on self-respect. Where "everything" is theoretically attainable, anything less than everything may be defined as failure. In earlier generations the definitions of success were modest and easily achievable. In the upwardly mobile society, what does one have to do to prove to either oneself or those around that one is a success? Whatever the rung on the ladder, why not the rung above? The inability to draw satisfaction from accomplishments in an open-ended society where there could always be more is a frustrating one. No one is necessarily rich enough; no one has enough security or power, and few people are prepared to call themselves a success in their internal reckonings.

The nature of work, moreover, has become distressingly diminished. There are few of us who can either bake a loaf of bread or make a pair of shoes. That capability of starting with nothing and ending with something is an enormously gratifying one, even though I will acknowledge that there may be monotony in always ending up with the same thing. But to work on the assembly line and always end up with something incomplete, to have added only one bolt to the same slot in a thousand incomplete parts of things is to be no longer a craftsman but a pseudo machine. And not a particularly good one at that. The Japanese are demonstrating that on the assembly line the machine is better than the person. The fragmentation of work and the dissociation of the worker's labor from his product reduce the capacity for pride in work. The robotization of labor removes work as a source of worth and self-esteem. Fragmented, assembly-line work is a slender reed with which to support a sense of security.

We are left with few such supports. The smaller our pool of resources for pride, the more protective we will be of any attempts to encroach on or undermine those few instruments of self-respect which remain. In our private lives, the withdrawal of love will preeminently threaten and anger us. In the public sector, where we expect no love, censure and disapproval will suffice.

THE EXPANDING POPULATION OF THE DEPRIVED

The egalitarian society still eludes us, and all current political states can distinguish within their populations a privileged and a deprived segment. We tend to judge a society in terms of the percentage of the population that is privileged, the disparity between the two groups, the method of selecting the privileged and the readiness of access to that group. In even the best society, however, the deprived will feel resentful and angry. We have within the last forty years or so in America managed to perversely maintain our deprived minorities while making our privileged majorities *feel* deprived.

During the Great Depression there was an extraordinary amount of true privation. People were without jobs, without means for decent housing and often without the necessary food to sustain themselves. Poverty was a generalized phenomenon, experienced across the entire spectrum of working people. The fear was palpable, but not the anger. What anger existed focused on the times, the system, the landlords, the bosses—with little resentment neighbor to neighbor. We were all in the same sinking boat.

I am neither minimizing the destructiveness nor romanticizing the state of poverty. Grinding poverty of an absolute nature is more degrading, corrupting and indecent than relative deprivation. It is dehumanizing and dispiriting; but as such, it is less likely to generate anger. The poverty of the underdeveloped countries produces a broken, passive population dominated by hopelessness and resignation. Anger is, at least, an emotion of defiance. It implies that the struggle continues. It is a step upward from submission and despair. It is only in the capacity to generate anger that relative deprivation seems more important.

A sense of deprivation thrives on differentials: when others have what we do not. We can endure the fact that we do not have something unless we feel that something has been taken away from us. We will then experience a sense of violation, of assault on our powers, which will ultimately be experienced as denigration. The smoldering rage that comes with feeling cheated is always present in deprivation. Who deprived us is not particularly important. We know deprivation when we see a disparity between that which we

have and that which we assume to be the standard a
Deprivation is a sociologically destructive feeling that
it a resentment which will not be contained but will sp
those who have cheated us, whom we may not know
who were not cheated and who thus in some unfathomable way will
be considered accomplices to our deprivation. From there we will
extend our resentment to the society which allowed us to be so
cheated.

I am using deprivation, therefore, in a way close to the way
Max Scheler used *"ressentiment"* in his masterly essay on that subject.[3] Scheler felt that *ressentiment* was a kind of "psychological
dynamite that contains within it the explosive rage that can destroy
any society." Inequitable societies could exist without *ressentiment*.
The key factor was not the standard of living or even an unfair
distribution of goods. Only where inequity exists in an *egalitarian*
society can *ressentiment* thrive. The determinant, according to
Scheler, was the *"discrepancy* between the political, constitutional or
traditional status of the group and its factual power. It is the
difference between these two factors that is decisive, not one of
them alone."[4] In other words, an individual can accept an under-
privileged status in a society that pretends to nothing other. The
danger arises when the society promises more than it delivers.

"Ressentiment must therefore be strongest in a society . . .
where approximately equal rights (political and otherwise) go hand
in hand with wide factual difference in power, property, and education."[5] The society Max Scheler was describing was Germany in
1912, but could indeed have been modern America.

I prefer the word "deprivation" to *ressentiment* because in En-
glish, at least, the concept of resentment has other implications.
The feeling of deprivation in our society derives from the fact the
system seems consistently to promise more to almost everybody
than it is capable of delivering. Perhaps it is promising too much.
Whenever a citizen feels that he has played according to the rules
and the reward is not forthcoming, he will feel duped and deprived.
That to which he is entitled has been taken away from him. He is
cheated and deprived, and the anger of that constellation of feelings
is profound. To go through life deprived is to go through life angry.

We live in a world of such disparities as to constitute almost an

143

embarrassment. The sybaritic life of the affluent compared with the standards of the poorest is an affront to conscience. Three short blocks from my office can lead to abject poverty or luxurious self-indulgence. The disparity is still not so great as that which exists in most underdeveloped countries of the world. But there is little promise there and less illusion. Where true privation exists—starvation, lack of shelter—deprivation is a luxury. The disparity here is also not necessarily greater than in those Marxist states which elevate egalitarianism over all other virtues, including liberty. There must be massive feelings of deprivation in the Marxist states. Without freedom, it is a stillborn feeling and can be left ignored by societies that found their security on the coercive power of the government rather than the loyalty of the people.

The feeling of deprivation goes beyond the material. If it were only in the material area, I suspect it would be limited in its effect in a society such as ours where even the worst-off are better off than the majority in other places and where some of the promise is always fulfillable. A generation of poverty may be tolerable to the black community, but after four generations of substandard existence—whatever the causes—the very possibility of access to the privileged position is despairingly questioned. It was the betrayal of the egalitarian promise of the New Deal and the expectations of the Great Society that directly led to a sense of deprivation. I do not know why we were incapable of fulfilling those promises. They still do not seem either grandoise or utopian. But they were not fulfilled. In this atmosphere deprivation can flourish even without privation —and there is never a shortage of the latter.

In addition, goods and things above the poverty threshold are supposed to produce pleasure. When they do not, we may create a sense of deprivation even in a privileged majority. When we feel deprived, beyond luxuries, of the very promise of life, we experience a loss that is close to despair. When we feel deprived of pleasure, we question the very value of existence.

We have managed to establish a somewhat pleasureless existence. Factors in the technological society conspire to erode our pleasure. Not knowing how to account for the lack of it, we displace it onto the material.

If we could afford a Mercedes, a house in East Hampton, a trip to St. Moritz, we would have pleasure. It is only because of our ignorance of these areas that we are free to romanticize them and maintain the illusion that somewhere in this society pleasure is abundant. We assume that if we continue the movement up the level of material accretions, we will finally locate pleasure hidden among the accumulated things.

But the same anhedonia dominates the beach clubs and the watering places of the rich; the penthouses are as lonely and sterile as are the tenement flats. I am not depreciating materialism. I am not being so foolish as to assume that money does not buy good things. It is pleasanter to eat at Lutèce than it is at Howard Johnson. The food is better, for one thing. But the diners at Lutèce have the same dispirited *ennui* as the diners at Howard Johnson—and perhaps more. When a HoJo regular is given the opportunity to dine at Lutèce, he may experience real pleasure, not just in the food, but in the sense of special privilege, in the delight of the extraordinary. The readily available, unfortunately, soon comes to seem ordinary even when, like oranges, it is truly special.

As long as there are appreciable material deprivation and the promise that it may someday be alleviated, we will tolerate the anhedonia of our life by falsely assuming that pleasure will arrive with our improved material status. By the time we have all achieved middle-class status, we cannot continue the deception. Money does *not* buy pleasure, even though its absence can surely generate pain.

By assuming that material things would buy happiness, we designed our goals in that direction. When the paths seemed to lead to no reward, we assumed we must traverse them still further. The assumption was wrong, but by the time we discovered that we had been driving ourselves down a path that led nowhere, we were too frightened, too discouraged, too exhausted to look for other roads to pleasure. We had already sacrificed our youth, our pleasure in the company of our children (who are no longer children and no longer surround us), our imagination and our undeveloped resources. We feel deprived at the most fundamental level. We feel robbed of the very meaning of existence. And we will rage at the irretrievable loss.

INEQUITY, UNFAIRNESS AND INJUSTICE

When this sense of deprivation ceases to be a transient phenomenon and when it is seen as the order of things, not just for oneself but for one's group, one's class, a majority of the people, it extends beyond the feeling of personal exploitation and into a sense of general disorder or corruption. "The system is not working." This sense of things' "not working" is one of the most terrifying of all in the social structure. The inequitable society is at least potentially correctable. It can mobilize us to efforts of improvement. Inequity is compounded when it is seen as calculated or even when it is simply seen as tolerated. If the disparity between treatment of groups is particularly marked: when blacks are treated differently from whites; men from women; white-collar criminals from blue-collar—there is legitimate outrage. When this is seen as a calculated policy, there is more than just personal outrage: there is a sense of intolerable exploitation and unbearable unfairness.

With the sense of unfairness we see how symbolic events which do not directly affect our daily existence can have profound social impact. The pardoning of the President who trampled on the basic trust of the people was an outrage to the average man. It was, perhaps, made tolerable by the punishment of the other principals in Watergate. Could the system have tolerated the pardoning of the entire group of Watergate offenders? We must feel that at least generally, we occupy a moral world if not a perfectly moral one. On average, good must triumph.

The obvious resentment, anger and fury of deprived minorities has been studied and discussed with great intelligence and sensitivity. That these studies have not necessarily corrected the inequity is another quite critical matter. A phenomenon that may be as dangerous and that remains to be studied is the alienation of a majority. The white American, middle-class or blue-collar, who has played by the rules is confused by and resentful of what he perceives as implicit attacks on himself in the context of ameliorating the condition of minorities. During the period when it was fashionable for blacks to disassociate themselves from all identity of class and work, the term "honky"—sanctioned by intellectuals—

146

became an accusation and a threat, to which the white working-class American responded with confusion, hurt, rage, hatred and eventually increased bigotry. He did not see himself as the enemy of anyone. He certainly did not see himself as a member of a privileged class. In his own way, through different sources, he was only too aware of his own vulnerability and the fragility of his own position. He had his own reasons for feeling deprived.

When not just the minorities, but the majority feels alienated, we are close to chaos. White blue-collar workers in America are beginning to feel that "the rules"—whatever they are—are not working; or worse, that the rules have been changed in the middle of the game. Or worse yet, that there are no rules. He has fulfilled his part of the bargain. He has sacrificed pleasure for position, respect and security and he has been deprived of all of these. It is more than deprivation, it is unfairness. "It's not fair!" is a statement of greater moral fervor and weight than "I don't have!" A good society may tolerate—may even do—bad things necessary to its survival. We will still identify a justice in its methods. A society that tolerates unfairness is not a good society. It serves injustice, and it will not command our support.

BETRAYAL

The difference between feeling deprived and feeling betrayed is often determined by one's identification. We are deprived by those others who have the power. We are betrayed by our own kind. The white middle class began to feel deceived and cheated. They had been seduced by promises not kept and then deserted. They had been led down the garden path. They had kept the faith and had still been delivered into the hands of the enemy. These phrases are all part of the language and definition of betrayal.

The betrayal felt by the white Americans may well have started in the sixties with the revolt of their own children. The reversal of values in the sixties seemed an assault on the standards of the parent. In the short-lived antimaterialism of the student revolt of the sixties the white middle class joined with the working class in the sense of outrage and betrayal. The material goods which their children affected to reject had been purchased by them at extraordinary cost. They had lived their lives doing unrewarding work, compensating with the assumption that somehow or other that which they bought with the earnings from that work was adequate reward for the drudgery they endured. In attacking their homes, their two-week vacations, their large automobiles, their children were challenging the trade-off their parents had made. Spitting on the flag was not all that outraged the parents; spitting on the twenty-one-inch color television set, the wall-to-wall carpeting, the patio furniture, the Radarange and the Buick was worse. The children were attacking a way of life for which their parents had paid dearly.

In addition, many of those parents saw these trappings of a middle-class lifestyle as the social sign of their upward progress from the Depression days of their childhood. While their children would choose to go barefoot they would recall the times when barefootedness was not an option but a shame and a statement of social caste. For children to affect the dress of the working class— the overalls, the work shoes—was a bewildering rejection of the very status symbols for which the parents had traded much of their pleasure and energy. In attacking these symbols the student revolution raised questions and doubts about the irrevocable contract the middle class had signed. It was too painful to acknowledge the possibility that they had opted for simply another mess of pottage.

The same deprivation minority groups had been feeling for years, stemming from the lesser share they were expected to accept, was now felt by the white middle class, although for different reasons. They received their proper share, but the value of that share was now suspect. Somehow or other the promise had been broken. Somehow or other the expectation had not been met. This general sense of betrayal contributed, and continues to contribute, to the mass resentment and anger in our culture.

FRUSTRATION

The sources of frustration in our society are immense, and resist cataloguing. They are most intense when they inhibit goals of work or love. One of the more unsettling sights is played out on television almost every spring. Within hours of the first announcement of registration for a few hundred available summer jobs, the television camera will record a line of literally thousands of mostly black teenagers queued up in anticipation. Many of them will have been in line the entire night. When the desire for work is frustrated, particularly in an adolescent, the frustration can lead to feelings of helplessness and anger. Any boy or girl who gets up the night before to sign up for a job ought to have a job—must have a job— and it is the responsibility of society to supply him with a job for both his self-respect and ours.

The unemployed black teenager fuses three problems: the problem of minority groups, the problem of adolescents and the problem of unemployment. Perhaps it is best to separate these three. Minority groups in particular suffer from a sense of deprivation. Whatever the causes—economic, sociological, political; beyond the discussions of this book—there remains the constant financial and social gap between Black and White. It is specious and unnecessary to point out that the black American is better off today than he was fifty years ago or that he is probably better off than the average black resident of most black countries. I am talking now of that feeling of frustration which stems from deprivation, and deprivation is not privation.

The emphasis on pure economics has been simplistic and has done a disservice to this problem. Admitting this is not a denial of the humiliation of grinding poverty. It is simply an affirmation of the equally destructive aspect of relative deprivation. To many white Americans, Watts did not seem a particularly hideous environment. This undermined the empathy felt by many white Americans who, confusing privation with deprivation, saw little difference between this neighborhood and their own. Deprivation, remember, is the distinction between what one assumes one ought to have—because it is deserved, it has been earned or promised— and that which is delivered.

There is a special kind of frustration when one's best is not enough and when the suggestion is that it never will be enough because of race. What is one to do? Despise oneself in acceptance of the judgment of inferiority? Refuse to accept the charge of essential inferiority and rage against the false accusation? Both have been tried and neither does more than compound the problem in a different way, although the latter at least salvages a modicum of self-respect. A derivative negative consequence of both is that either can allow for a total abdication of responsibility for one's condition by supplying a ready rationalization for all failure, thus blunting self-examination and the guilt that prods to action.

Racism cuts both ways, and with every stroke it is hacking at the lifelines of our society. We have managed to live with this problem too long. We are accommodating to it. Like the symptoms of a chronic disease, it no longer seems as seriously discommoding. It is now so constant a factor in our daily existence that like the smog and the filth in the streets, it has become an unnoticed part of the familiar landscape of our lives. We have made progress, but the pace, somehow and in some yet undiscovered way, *must* be picked up. Other frustrating conditions of our society are increasing the level of resentment and rage at an alarming rate and demanding new attention. The increase in alienation and anger, if not just simple justice, demands a renewed assault on the problem of prejudice.

The adolescent presents a peculiar and special minority. Biologically, human beings are forced to spend an exceptional amount of time in the dependency period. If one assumes that sexual maturity —the capacity to reproduce one's own kind—is reached at fourteen or fifteen, the years preceding it represent 25 percent of what had been a natural life expectancy of sixty. One of our solutions to the problem of biological dependency has been to extend our life expectancy, thus increasing the percentage of postdependent years.

If, instead of the age of biological reproduction, one dates maturity from the age when one achieves the capacity to fulfill the adult role (worker, father, mother, member of the community), it might be seen as somewhere between eighteen and twenty-one, or roughly a third of the natural life expectancy. No animal even approaches these outrageous figures. A dog is able to reproduce at nine months and has a life expectancy of twelve to fifteen years and is a full adult with all of its powers by a year and a half—some 10 percent of its expected life span. We are an exceptional species.

Human beings remain in childhood for a particularly long time. Being a child has many implications. It means we are assigned less responsibility, and that we are entitled to the care which is afforded dependents. It also has negative implications. Being a child means being less than an adult. With less responsibility there is less authority—and less power. This is particularly difficult to endure for the adolescent, who often feels at the peak of his power well prior to the granting of his full authority by society.

What have we done with this peculiar biology? We have managed to intensify and compound the problem by culturally *prolonging* the dependency period. We have managed to take "childhood" and sociologically extend it far beyond the biological age range in which it is normally manifest. The human male is generally capable of sexual performance at the age of twelve to fifteen, but up to the recent sexual revolution, we had penalized adolescent sexual behavior by inducing fear and guilt. The guilt was inequitably spread. It was the young woman who was made to feel guilty. The young man was controlled by other means; while permitted sexual activity, he was forced to separate his sexual appetite from love, and he carried the scars of that mandate into his mature years.

There were good reasons for discouraging adolescent sexual involvement in a day when birth control was difficult to enforce or encourage. Certainly the teenage child is ill prepared, in our current complex culture, for the adult role of a parent. In a simpler society, a rural society dominated by the family farm, there was at least a rough congruence between achieving biological and cultural or sociological maturity. In an age of technology, however, more training is necessary to fulfill the role of even the average adult. We have come well beyond the needs of the three R's. And it has been only in the past few "moments" of our evolution that formal education was invented, let alone seen as a necessary instrument of survival.

We define "childhood" in terms of this first dependency period and have managed to extend it into the twenties, and for those who are becoming professionals, into the thirties. The student role is generally seen as a child's role, and the number of adult-by-almost-any-standard students is increasing. We have created a kind of

monster child-adult, which may in part explain the periodic eruptions of dissatisfaction in student populations.

It is humiliating and frustrating to have the acknowledgment
of one's adulthood deferred to such an advanced age. The dependent
role carries with it all the other implications of dependency—
helplessness, powerlessness, immaturity. In addition, in our male-
oriented society not to be seen as an adult has special implications
for the men. The relationship of "man" to "boy" is different from
the relationship of "woman" to "girl." To be a "man" is emotionally charged in a society that equates masculinity with power and
authority. Dependency for the male is being denied not just adulthood but manhood and masculinity, with all the dangerous implications of that deprivation. It reduces self-respect and can drive the
adolescent to behavior designed to disprove his childishness, his
lack of power and his general impotence.

While we need more knowledge to function in a technological
world, we have been insensitive to some of the implications of this
prolongation of dependency. We have approached such problems as
employment of the adolescent as if they were luxuries, secondary to
employment of the adult, rather than recognizing that it may be
just as necessary for adolescents to support a failing self-esteem.
Some means to limit the expansion of the dependency period must
be found. It may be necessary to redefine the role of the student by
making it a form of career and paying one for this career, thus
establishing this as an independent profession. The European Talmudists were so treated by the Jewish ghetto communities. Much
of the turmoil we define as adolescent behavior may be only a
cultural artifact rather than a biological determinant.

If unemployment is a problem for the adolescent, at least it is
part and parcel of a role which also has its benefits (lower expectations and lesser responsibilities), even if those are not often explicitly appreciated by the adolescent. Unemployment in the adult,
particularly the adult male, whose entire pride has been vested in
areas of work and mastery (as distinguished from love and attachment), causes a more dangerous frustration that leads to humiliation. The pictures of laid-off workers in the mill towns across the
country are not just images of men who are frightened for their
survival. They are images of shamed and angry men. These work-

ing-class men defined their worth and self-respect in simple terms. They were to bring home the weekly paycheck. They would then have fulfilled their obligation to society, and beyond that to their children and their wives. One's work was the major part of the definition of "man." One's work fulfilled his obligations as husband and father. Even when insurance benefits sustained men during unemployment, one saw the shame in their miens and one sensed the guilt and anger that accompanied it.

These are men who want to work. They are being frustrated in the basic desire for mastery and achievement. They have been deprived through no fault of their own of that which our culture has defined as the criterion of success. When they have worked for twenty-five years in an industry that seemed as solid and secure as the steel industry once did, and then find themselves out of jobs, they are hurt and bewildered. And when the mill shuts down, foreclosing any hope of reemployment, they experience frustration at its most extreme. This is true whether the unemployed worker is white or black, but with the latter it will be still another assault on his self-respect. The mounting population of the chronically unemployed is as dangerous an accretion as any chronic poison in our environment.

Of course, female frustration in the area of work was not even identified as a problem until very recently. The fact that women's assigned cultural role did not even acknowledge their right to the pride of mastery in work went unattended. For years, either those women who did work were viewed as idiosyncratic, or their work was a sign of depreciated social status—implying a failure; suggesting their inability to attract a man who could adequately support them. For the most part women found the creativity of work through their efforts as homemakers and mothers, although many resented the disparaging lack of value placed on those two roles.

Even feminists commit the error of ennobling the traditional work of men over the traditional work of women. It is not necessarily the nature or intrinsic value of men's work that is better, but the value placed on it and the rewards for it. Work for the average person is drudgery, satisfying needs of pride and economics, not pleasure.

The absence of a primary joy in work (as distinguished from

pride in working) has existed for many years. It was accelerated by the fragmentation of work that accompanied the Industrial Revolution. A craftsman and a farmer can still produce a whole and useful product. There are few of these individual workers left. Even farmers are likely to work on assembly-line farms, and the absence of craftsmen is evident in the inability to find a reliable automobile or watch repairman, let alone find a cobbler who can make a pair of shoes, or any individual who actually builds a total thing.

The typical work in our society is neither rewarding nor ennobling. In a suburban setting it is particularly ironic to hear women discussing the triviality of their work as compared with that of their husbands. At one such gathering I analyzed what the women present did in the course of their day. They raised the next generation and supplied them with their values. They ran the school system. They operated the local political machinery, often serving in elective office. They organized the charities and developed the cultural aspects of the community. Their husbands, in the meantime, were doing the "important things." They worked for advertising agencies persuading people to drink one cola rather than another. They were tax lawyers and accountants helping the rich to retain their riches. When even privileged occupations afforded so little gratification, what were women aspiring to? Surely it was not the joy of mining coal or being a toll collector or shoveling manure that fostered the sense of deprivation.

The distinction between women and men was not in the nature of their assigned work. The difference was in the power and respect granted each role and in the way that these two things are converted into self-respect.

There is contempt for the traditional role that we assign to women—and women know it and suffer from it—and there is little pay and little privilege that goes with it. Work, then, independent of its real value, is primarily a title of rank and an instrument of power. I would much rather be a mother tending my children than a pediatrician who must drearily sit all day long examining other people's healthy babies, *if* the pay were as good, the prestige were as great, the respect were there and the power that accrues from these things were vested in me. Knowing that this is not so, I would of course infinitely prefer the less than stimulating (to me) job as the pediatrician. And so would many women.

HUMILIATION

The increased insecurity generated by all the conditions discussed mobilizes our emergency emotions, generating quantities of fear and anger with little adaptive value. These emotions are painfully intensified if our inadequacies should be exposed to the public view. To be impotent is painful enough. To have one's powerlessness exposed is the ultimate announcement of just how helpless we truly are. Public exposure is the ultimate humiliation. When we announce our contempt for the power of others, when we institutionalize such contempt, these "others" feel the rage and frustration of the desperate. The back-of-the-bus phenomenon was a destructive institution beyond its simple unfairness. The public sanction of racism was the heel on a head already in the dust.

Bias and prejudice may exist as extensively as they once did, but the fact that we dare not, often under penalty of law, advertise our bias or contempt is still a giant step forward. Fair-minded individuals who condemned the humiliating aspect of such public symbols as separate toilets, or the subtler depreciation involved in the white Southerner's refusal to use such common forms of address as "Mr." or "Mrs." toward blacks, often seem particularly insensitive to the similar forms of public depreciation that involve women. Why does a secretary bridle when a male employer asks her to get him a cup of coffee and uses a term like "honey"? It may be an acceptable way to ask a wife for coffee at home in the morning. (It may not be so nice for the wife either if it is always the man who is doing the asking.) But the same request, utilizing the same language, has a profoundly different meaning when transferred into the office and invested in the relationship of an employer, in a position of power, to his secretary, in a position of vulnerability. The person is not his honey, and utilizing terms of endearment is a duplicitous means of establishing a dependent relationship. It is the dependence of subservience, not the mutual dependence of love.

We have done away with many of the caste distinctions of dress and even language. Workers no longer deferentially tip their hats to the upper classes. It is difficult these days to distinguish by appearance workman from employer, particularly among the young. Progress has been made. Nonetheless, there is a dangerous tendency to underestimate the small slight in public. Slights are never small when they are exposed to an onlooker. The ethnic joke must not be considered funny. The conservative who will *correctly* interpret the graffiti on public buildings and streets and subways as a sign of the deterioration of common values and of contempt for the public space will tend to minimize the graffiti of the mind and the graffiti of the soul. At the same time, the liberal who will be vigilant in protecting against racial and ethnic slurs has in the past romanticized the abuse of physical graffiti by endowing them with some obscure charm or artistic relevance. Both forms of graffiti are public shows of contempt for people or public space. Both are forms of intimidation and humiliation, and neither ought to go unchecked.

CYNICISM AND DESPAIR

In the history of civilization we have endured the inequities and frustrations of unjust societies with the assurance that they too would pass. And they did. The temples of Ozymandias and the Colosseums of the Caesars are defunct. In addition, when we once all shared a religious conviction of the order and rightness of things under God's authority, we did not care what temporal injustices we might be required to endure. It was all part of His plan. This brief life on earth was but an evanescent stage on a journey toward a better life beyond. By now most of us have abandoned hopes of heaven and see no evidence of a Beulah Land. We expect our rewards right here on earth. We want justice now. If there is injustice and the good suffer while the bad prosper, then why be good? If the rules do not work then why follow the rules? A pervasive sense of injustice is the parent of anger and cynicism.

Even in humiliation there is hope of restitution. As with most other painful emotional states, the very pain of the experience drives us to behavior to correct the condition that is generating the feeling. It is true that in the desperation of humiliation the actions taken may be violent; gratuitous; not even necessarily directed at the source of the humiliation. But at least, as with the neurotic symptom, it is the sign of a struggling—and therefore still vital and viable—creature. When cynicism leads us to despair, we collapse, as in depression, into acceptance of our diminished state and our disrepaired world. Even in depression, however, there is an underlying plea for help. One sees the patient desperately reducing himself with the unconscious expectation that if he is reduced sufficiently, he will be picked up like a child and nurtured into health.

It is a sign of the desperation and cynicism of our time that we have revived this primitive dependency adaptation. Too many of us are hoping that someone will appear and take us in hand, that somehow or other we will be picked up and restored. Barely hidden beneath our apparent current contempt for authority is a *hunger* for authority ready to be exploited. The readiness of many in our population to accept false prophets cuts across gender, class, race and wealth. The religious cults and the therapeutic religions are signs of the desire for a quick fix. It is frightening to observe the transformation of the political process into an almost purely charismatic enterprise—abetted, of course, by television.

We have lost our faith in ideas and principles. We have become apolitical. We have abdicated. We no longer assume responsibility. We are ready for a dependency solution. We are looking for Big Daddy, the smiling, paternalistic father who speaks gently, demands little and promises much. We are ready for simplistic answers and jingoistic cures. Anyone who promises to recognize our slights, to correct our humiliations, to justify our rage, to restore our potency, to increase our self-respect, to punish those who are depriving us and to restore us to our birthright will be listened to. He will be listened to and followed.

The anger of dispossessed minorities now joined with the anger of a majority invites tension and anomie. That we rage implies that we still resist—and gives us the small comfort of time to make rectification. But the anger itself poses a risk. The problems inherent in a postatomic culture are complex enough without the burdens of a ubiquitous and nonadaptive rage.

8. The Obsolescence of Anger

Perhaps we should not change our culture. Perhaps we should adjust our expectations. Other people have lived more brutal lives in more hostile communities. Stability requires neither *politesse* nor grace. We could accommodate our culture to tolerate our anger. In a sense, that is precisely what we have done, without a calculated decision. Where survival seemed to require a certain degree of brutalization and coarsening of sensitivity, we accepted that price. We may even eventually condone and ennoble paranoid and competitive characteristics.

In 1968 Napoleon Chagnon[1] described a people and a culture whose values managed to completely reverse Western concepts of good and evil. The Yanomamo Indians of southern Venezuela are a people who operate socially in a constant state of rage, with high volatility and quick, fiery tempers. A short fuse, a low flash point and a readiness to use violence at the slightest provocation are considered virtues in their culture. The Yanomamo act according to a set of rules as well defined as ours. Decorum must be observed. Proper social behavior is expected and respected. By their own standards these people are neither cruel nor antisocial. Virtue in their culture, as in ours, is defined by the accommodation of behavior to an implicit and explicit code of conduct.

158

The Yanomamo not only live in a chronic state of warfare with their neighbors, they incorporate the lessons of violence and aggression into their domestic lives. Their wives must be beaten to demonstrate the male capacity for violence. Their political and social behavior is dominated by flamboyant shows of aggression. Boasts of one's own prowess are *de rigueur* and are presented in a context of continual intimidation and exaggeration of one's own personal strength. The Yanomamo is not only prepared to be angry, he seeks ways to test the boiling point of those with whom he deals. At the Feast of the Allies the men throw insults at each other and engage in chest-pounding and side-slapping duels that seem almost an imitation of the power-announcing behavior of apes.

These are not instances of idle or random behavior. Since the society sees itself as dependent for survival on aggressiveness, aggression must be supported and encouraged and Yanomamo men must display ferocity. The chest-pounding, side-slapping and club-fighting are regulatory mechanisms to prevent either all-out war or the internal destruction of the social order.

The Yanomamo seem to have a stable society, but it is a homogeneous society. The rules are explicit; they are the same for all, and all conform. But what about the Yanomamo among ourselves? Many in our society, more often men than women, also operate with a short fuse and a readiness to anger. Their pugnacious proclivity is advertised in manners somewhat more subtle than chest-pounding and side-slapping but just as explicit.

Within the family context the short fuse may be as effective and perhaps as stabilizing an influence in our society as it is among the Yanomamo. It sets a standard of behavior, although an autocratic, brutal and unfair one. But as with the number of lions on the mountain, there is room for only one male Yanomamo to a household.

In the external world these lions are less effective. It is unlikely that our society could work by extending much further the limits of tolerable rage. The social scenes in which aggressive, overtly expressed anger and inclination toward violence are effective are extremely limited. Perhaps in a teenage gang, where a pecking order may be established by one's readiness to risk one's life in combat; perhaps in a motocycle club or some other idiosyncratic subculture of violence; but not in the general society. We give them distance, these Yanomamo who dwell among us, because of their snarling nature, but we make them pay for their surliness and intimidation of us. The impulsive release of anger, particularly with the intention of advertising it to those around us, has very little utilitarian value in a culture where power is more readily evidenced by dollar signs than by muscle mass. Very few of our conflicts these days are resolved by biting and wrestling matches. Certainly by now the evidence is clear that rage rarely has an adaptive value.

We have learned by experience not to trust some of the emotional signals of stress that are generated by our physiology. Responding to the typical threats in a technological society by immediate physical attack is usually foolish and ineffective. Beyond that, we have learned that a threatening situation may be so only in our perception. Why, then, the current cult of catharsis; why the overvaluation of direct and overt expression of anger? I have suggested that it derives in part from our misreading of early psychoanalytic theory in which catharsis was seen as a cure for neuroses, and by extension we developed a cathartic theory of therapeutics.

We live in a society dominated by therapeutic models of behavior. We are almost obsessed with expanding the concept of health to include all aspects of life. Happiness has ceased to be a justifiable aspiration. We feel more comfortable seeking happiness under the rubric of health. It seems less self-indulgent to seek treatment than to seek pleasure. If we want something, we go to the doctor, and we call that which we want a cure for an illness. But what is the name of that illness for which the treatment is a hair transplant, a transsexual operation, a tushy-tuck or a breast enlargement? The early psychiatric assumption that catharsis would cure mental illness was false. Even if it had been correct, the existential anger of modern life is not the same as the irrational anger that feeds neuroses, and would not necessarily respond to this treatment, or to any "treatment." Neurosis implies an internal and irrational set of adjustments. Social anger may be only too rational and justifiable.

Another factor that may have contributed to the popularity of the cathartic model was exhaustion with, and disappointment in, the rules of the essentially WASP culture in which we live. We have been trained to bide our time, to be patient, to be temperate, to be civilized. The assumption must always have been there that this would produce a decent and rewarding life. If it does not, then what? Then there will be the anger of betrayal, the rage over the promise not kept.

The "have-nots" assumed that if they behaved themselves the "haves" would share—but the "haves" did not. The "haves" in turn discovered that what they had was not all that satisfying. Maturity, they were told, lay in the recognition that one must delay immediate and superficial gratification to ensure the more profound pleasures of the future. To defer immediate pleasures for long-range pleasures which never arrive is an outrage that will compound all the anger we contained in the process of our becoming mature. Why bother holding anything back?

It also may be that in a society with so much frustration, containment became progressively more difficult. We serve our pride when we rationalize the inevitable by labeling it desirable. The pain of constant confrontation with one's impotence, inadequacy and unrealized gratifications may have demanded a rationalization of the simple pleasure of raging at the events.

Another element that may have led to ennobling the concept of expressed anger may be that in one context, within the intimacy of loving relationships, expression is often effective. The relative value of directly expressing one's angry feeling will always vary with the relationship between the angry person and the source of his anger.

In the household there should be an atmosphere of nourishment and love and of shared destinies. It is also an environment of continuity. The same people will occupy the same space on a reasonably permanent basis. In addition, in intimate relationships all responses are mitigated, modified or enhanced by the peculiar conditions of identification. If someone I love is hurt, it is the equivalent of my being hurt and is an offense which I am unlikely to forgive. I am unlikely to forgive it even if I am the person who hurts the someone I love. Similarly, if I feel damaged by a loved one it would be as wrong to maintain decorum with that loved one as it would be to express those same feelings to a chance acquaintance. The purpose at home is not the temporary maintenance of an ephemeral peace. The "moment" must be subservient to the longer term. It is the ongoing relationship that is important. Even within the family, the expression of anger will vary in effectiveness with the character of the person expressing it, the character of the person to whom the anger is addressed, the state and nature of their relationship and the symbolic meanings with which they will endow the anger.

I remember hearing of a personal disagreement between a wife and husband. The wife could not believe that after having shared a long and happy married life, her husband operated under an emotional system so differently adjusted from hers. The event that precipitated the discussion was one of those knock-down arguments which occur so infrequently in the living rooms of well-mannered people. The woman had let a friend "have it." The person who received the attack had earned it many times over. A passive-aggressive person, she had been baiting the wife all evening. She was reduced to tears by the wife's honest expression of her dissatisfaction with and anger at such behavior.

Later the couple discussed the event. The wife was almost manic in her feelings. Her husband was shocked. He was miserable. He had seen no purpose to the confrontation, and anticipated their next meeting with embarrassment. What purpose had been served? Who had needed to reduce this friend to tears? She would never learn to change her behavior. She was as she was.

It was clear that the wife had the justifying and rectifying experience of having righted a wrong, of having put things in order. After politely and silently tolerating her own exploitation by the other woman for some time, she had finally seen an opportunity arrive to clear the air; attack the cant, hypocrisy and self-deception; let the woman have some of her own back. She felt cleansed and delighted—and her husband was personally shocked to hear how she had "enjoyed" the scene of the other woman in tears.

She in turn could not believe that he was miserable. She kept prodding him to "admit" that he had really enjoyed it too. To this day I am not sure she believes him when he says he did not. After all, how could two people with such common values and a lifetime of shared experience respond so differently? The explanation is that guilt holds such a dominant position in the husband's conscience that it undermines his pleasure in a clean and self-righteous show of rage. It might even be, partly, a distinction in gender. As a man, he had lost his temper frequently when younger and been capable of lashing out physically. Such physical assaults had carried with them the potential for real harm. The wife had never been in a physical fight in her life.

It may also have been related to birth order. He was the eldest of three sons. While the age difference between himself and his siblings was sufficient to obviate the violent physical fights characteristic of brothers closer in age, there had inevitably been times of struggle.

Given the four-year age difference between himself and the brother who was next in line, there had literally been no contest. This meant that his angers, when converted into physical terms, had invariably led to victories. He had been destined always to win. The effect was precisely the same as if he had been assured of always losing. There was no joy in victory. It was humiliating to have beaten up someone so obviously slighter, smaller, younger and less powerful.

The same could be said for conflicts of a nonphysical nature. To best someone who is obviously a child in relationship to oneself through verbal means, trickery, deception or cunning was similarly likely to engender guilt rather than gratification.

The wife, on the other hand, was the younger of two siblings. Bedeviled by a brother who was stronger and a year older, she had been subject to abuse with little chance of winning. When she did mobilize herself to lash back, victories *were* a source of pride. She overcame the odds of gender, size and age, and there had been sweetness and self-satisfaction and self-aggrandizement in such victories. Surely these factors played a role in their differing attitudes toward competitive victory.

Venting of spleen is only occasionally effective within the family, and rarely outside it. Our relationship to those strangers who accidentally inhabit the same public spaces as ourselves is quite different from our relationship with our family in our private spaces. They are governed by different sets of rules. Actions that are effective and indicated in one area are totally out of place in the other. I need not love, or necessarily know, the people I meet by chance in the post office, restaurant or market. They need not esteem me or forgive me my transgressions, since no need for love exists between us.

Those of us not bound together by the conditions of love and affection, nonetheless, must have some code of conduct to facilitate an amiable, if transient and superficial, relationship. We need a modus vivendi, an operative set of forms and manners that will permit us to share the public spaces for the purposes for which they are intended. The rules must be different from those in the family. That which is essential to ensure an ongoing relationship is not necessary when we are unlikely to meet again. That which is effective under the special rules of love will not even work with a stranger. It does me little good to sulk in your presence in the supermarket line; nor, conversely, need I forgive you your bad manners by understanding that which contributed to them. I am not your husband, your colleague or your psychoanalyst.

What is of prime importance in the public space is behavior, not motivation. We do not care why you choose to spit on the floor any more than we are concerned about your reasons for being rude and insulting. We want none of it. To vent your spleen in public is as much a form of public littering as if you chose to distribute your garbage there. It *is* a form of garbage. You have no right to let it all hang out, since that "out" in which you are hanging it is ours as well as yours. Save both your anger and your contrition for areas in which they have validity. Decorum in the public spaces must be maintained.

Failure to distinguish between the public and private spheres has caused much confusion about the value of expressing anger. It may explain why intelligent people can take such opposing positions. They are in all probability operating from a different context and then erroneously generalizing about all behavior from their different specifics. The textual framework will determine the propriety of the behavior. Psychologists generally have preached a message encouraging one to expose anger because they tend to deal with problems that arise in family relationships. In this area one should err in that direction more often than not. But even within the context of a loving relationship there are times for silence. There is a use of candor that is nothing less than cruel. The obligation to tell the truth does not extend to a requirement to announce the truth. There are even conditions that call for lying. There is no relationship so intimate and so trusting that it cannot be damaged by callous candor. All that can be safely said in terms of the release or containment of anger is the generalization that when in doubt, contain it in public, and in private spaces feel freer to release it.

We may continue testing the limits of our society's tolerance for angry frustration. I suspect we still have significant margins of safety. But I see no promise in converting the American culture into the Yanomamo. Sooner or later, by anyone's standard, we will have reached the tolerable limit of social anger. The unavoidable and essential problem rests in the obsolescence of physiological anger in a society in which power and survival are no longer founded on the physical. The solution begins with a full acknowledgment of what that obsolescence means. It may be simpler to approach the emotional issue of anger by examining briefly a parallel chemical example.

When that first slippery creature slithered from the sea to establish a terrestrial kingdom he took with him the vestiges of his marine existence. Now, after millions of years of evolution, the residual link with the oceans remains within that most advanced of all terrestrial species, the human being. The blood that circulates within us and nourishes every aspect of our existence has its salinity fixed at the level of seawater and it must be maintained at that level for life processes to continue. Elaborate mechanisms maintain this homeostatic balance. When we excrete large quantities of water through our sweat glands to cool ourselves in the heat of the day, the regulatory apparatus of the body operates to make sure that the concentration of sodium does not rise to a dangerously high level. We absorb fluid from our tissues and concentrate our urine so that less water is lost in the process of the elimination of waste. These are but two of the many devices our body has of maintaining this crucial balance. One other device is the thirst for water. Without any measurement or even knowledge of the sodium concentrations of the blood, when it is too high we experience a sensation of discomfort called thirst that is the primary stimulus to drink.

The availability of salt could not be assured for those first terrestrial animals, once they had abandoned the oceans. To ensure a proper level of this vital element, sodium, a specific hunger for salt was "built in" via evolution. Derrick Denton, in his extraordinary book *The Hunger for Salt,*[2] describes how that vestigial mechanism of defense may be in the process of destroying us. The hunger for salt seems to have a life of its own, independent of any need for sodium, which is now in ready supply. Salt's implication in high blood pressure and related diseases is apparent and has been for some time. This is a simple example of the extraordinary ability of our culture to destroy in an infinitesimally small amount of time the adaptive value of a device that was developed and nurtured over hundreds of millions of years.

For a million years or more our human ancestors survived the assault of the predators that stalked and threatened them through their strength and their wits. When they were frightened their intelligence guided them to methods of abrupt flight and cover that were not readily available to simpler animals. Their intelligence, goaded by their anger, devised instruments of destruction that permitted them to destroy animals for which they were no match physically. But what of the years that inevitably existed before our special intelligence could develop weapons of attack and instruments of defense? The time was bought by a physiology suited for survival. Fear and anger mobilized our bodies for flight or fight. The mechanism of anger made sure that when we attacked we were at our fittest. Blood was properly distributed, the appropriate muscles tensed, endocrines and sphincters adjusted to enhance and ensure the maximum effort. What maximum effort of sinew or muscle is necessary these days? What threats are solved by a clean and direct physical assault?

The physiology of rage, like the hunger for salt, still abides within us, and occasionally even prudence will be overpowered by biology. I recall an incident that took place some years ago. I was within three blocks of my office north of that previously described boundary at 96th Street. Three teenage boys were walking toward me. The larger two took the third and shoved him with some force so that he hurtled into me, almost knocking me down. I was annoyed and angry, but I was not about to get involved. I continued walking on my way. I noticed that the boys had turned around and were now beginning to taunt me. Crude, tough, smart-assed, they were trying to provoke me into anger, and I was determined to be prudent and avoid it. The boy who had been driven into me came right up to me and said he expected an apology. I turned away, swallowing my rage. A group of store owners were lounging around observing the scene. No one stepped forward to discourage the boys or establish an alliance with me. I think the incident in all likelihood would have ended there. The boys would have won their game. I had been successfully humiliated. At that moment, however, the smallest of the three, in one final insult, put his hand on my shoulder and said, "Next time, man, you'd better learn to apologize."

I suspect it was the laying on of the hand that made the difference and broke through my reserve. I wheeled and with all the pent-up rage contained within me grabbed him by the shirt, pulled him nose to nose and, spitting into his face, told him if he so much as touched me one more time I would beat him into the ground.

They walked away. It was, after all, only a game for them. I assume that I was not actually foaming at the mouth, but that is the image I carried away from that scene. My expression of rage was a stupid and foolish action; a vestige from boyhood, when one had to learn to "defend oneself" and a physical line, once drawn, had to be crossed. In retrospect I was shaken and upset by my lack of control. I had proved nothing. I needed to prove nothing to those boys. By accident of fortune I happened to have met three boys who were unarmed and at that moment uninterested in more aggressive behavior. At another time I could have had a knife in my ribs. In this case I may have won the day, but I actually won very little, and statistically my response had been more likely to put me in the hospital. I had no more control over that anger at that moment than does the cornered and wounded animal in the jungle.

In the early days of our evolution anger obviously served to alert, motivate and invigorate us in the battles to come. Some commentators insist that it still does. The social theorist Ernest

Becker says, "These aggressions are still 'in the service of the organism' because they represent a reaction to feeling cheated, duped, stripped naked, undermined. A person . . . reacts to assert himself, to show and feel he is someone to reckon with. Anger generally has this function for the person and is a way of setting things in balance once again."[3] Yet I fail to see how anger remains in the service of survival if it affects one's response to criticism from a superior and causes him to lose his job. He may have had a momentary flush of victory in getting his own back, but it cannot be considered to be in the service of *survival* to lose one's job to satisfy one's ego or vanity.

Psychiatrist David Hamburger, answering Becker, insists: "Emotional responses are not limited to behavior that facilitates reproductive success in contemporary human populations. Any mechanism [once adaptive] . . . may become largely maladaptive when there are drastic changes in environmental conditions. . . . some of the mechanisms which evolved during the millions of years of mammalian, primate and human evolution are less useful than they once were."[4] I think this is a conservative and minimal answer. The truth goes beyond this. It is not simply that the mechanisms of anger are less useful: they are positively destructive.

Even in response to a physical attack, the emergency emotion of anger rarely serves a useful purpose anymore. The assailant is usually better prepared to inflict injury than his victim. If fear had been my only response on 96th Street, I would have done the intelligent thing and run. Certainly fear was present. Anger dominated in the end. If anger is not useful even in the exceptional case when we are physically attacked, then what possible good can it serve in the more typical symbolic areas previously described where most threats currently occur? "Don't get mad, get even" is certainly a more rational, if not admirable, motto for survival these days.

The psychophysical response that served so effectively to defend the small clan, that ensured the dominance of the superior male in the hierarchy, that captured limited food supplies in times of famine and dominated the water hole offers precious little help with the competition in the law office, in dealing with delays at the airport or in responding to an unappreciative and nagging employer. If when waiting in line one finds that—naturally—one is in the longest and slowest line and the person at the head of the line seems a congenital idiot who speaks and understands no language known to man, the anger that is generated is totally inappropriate. While the person is considering whether it is tactical or wise to shift lines at this point, his physiology is considering how best to avoid extinction. His biology is sending signals appropriate for a life-threatening situation when only time is being killed. This is a ridiculous overreaction. Since most anger in modern life arises from events that are essentially trivial, although symbolically profound, we are constantly overresponding. Our bodies are preparing us for life-and-death struggles that exist only in our unconscious and in our physiology.

Possibly the very feeling of anger is the product of the physiology; it may be that without those alerting physiological responses, we would not even experience the feeling. This theory was first proposed by William James, and while unfashionable for some time, it has recently been revived. Even if the emotion is not the product of the physiology, however, the two are so fused that the intensity of one influences the other. A reciprocal relationship exists that compounds the maladaptive effect. The inappropriate quality and nature of the rage response—preparation for a life-threatening attack—dictates an inappropriate quantity of angry feeling. But the excess amount of anger reciprocally generated may force us to distort reality, to exaggerate the nature of the threat, to rationalize and act on the excessive rage we are experiencing.

If, for example, a man is treated rudely by a surly clerk in a haberdashery department, the excessive physiological response may force him to overvalue his sense of the injury done by the casual rudeness. He may then exaggerate the nature of the slight to make it conform to the quantity and quality of internal change. A paranoid elaboration will allow him to do precisely this—to see an offense at a department store, or in an automobile, as more than just characteristic rudeness: as an assault on his masculinity. He will feel "screwed." This, and like symbols of homosexual assault, used by men when they feel humiliated, indicates the sense of violation, castration and impotence that can be attached to even minor affronts if they are perceived as attacks on "manhood." The occasional violent eruptions in the city streets—often involving automobiles—are testament to this capacity for escalation. Men have been killed in New York City in arguments over parking spaces.

When the escalation of an affront is displaced from the personal to the political arena it is particularly frightening. When a population that has every reason to feel impotent and unsure of its worth is mobilized by a leader who shares these feelings of inadequacy, and who is in a position to act them out in games much more dangerous than those which have been described, the result can threaten the survival of us all.

We have come through a frightening period in which a disproportionate number of the world's leaders have proved to be men trapped in their own power struggles. A Hitler or Mussolini, strutting in uniform and acting out paranoid fantasies, is, of course, frightening. But the danger existed beyond these flagrant examples. With the emergence of the political memoirs and the biographies of respected world leaders who dominated the power structure of recent times comes a disturbing sense of how much pathology was contained beneath the public stance. The actions of Stalin, Churchill, Lyndon Johnson and Richard Nixon, to name but a few, raise questions of whether, or to what degree, a person in a position of leadership is capable of separating his personal feelings of pride, anxiety, intimidation, anger and humiliation from the national purpose.

Too many take great pleasure in the arbitrary use of power as a way of protecting against their feelings of impotence. I recall a particular incident vividly. I was on my way home and noticed to my delight I would just make an earlier train, the 5:10, than I had anticipated. This is one of the small triumphs of urban life. As I was just about to enter the gate to the train, however, a young trainman with long blond hair slammed the gate down. I pointed out to him that it was only 5:08. "It is five ten and that is when the gate closes," he responded. I showed him the clock on the wall of the station and he said the clock was slow. I continued the discussion with him and he sullenly said, "Why don't you go take your complaints to the stationmaster?" I was infuriated and helpless, and he knew it. Even if it had been 5:10, he had seen me running; why would it not have been more natural to hold up the gate a few moments to allow a straggler in? I could not understand his behavior. Rather than show my anger I simply asked him, "Why do you behave this way?" He looked at me and answered, "Because I enjoy it."

He did enjoy it. Opening and closing gates all day is not necessarily the most satisfying job. I have no idea what gratifications he derived from his work beyond that of earning an honest living. Was there anything intrinsic to the work that pleased or enhanced his ego or supported the sense of a superior self? Perhaps the only way he could obtain satisfaction and pride and a sense of power or achievement in his job was to slam the gate in the face of those who are always presumed to have been dealt a better hand.

What about powerful men and their frustrations? What about senators and Presidents and generals? I do not know how they manage with their internalized anger constantly sending them false signals that they are in danger, forcing them to confront a physiology attuned to survival in a sociological situation that is simply one of inconvenience. I am frightened by the games they might play to support their failing sense of power.

What can we do beyond recognizing that we are trapped in a vestigial and maladaptive emotional system? In this golden age of scientific advances, direct physiological intervention might seem an intriguing option. Either through pharmacological or through genetic methods yet to be developed we could assist our physiology in catching up with our psychosocial reality. Many intelligent people display a stubborn and often illogical resistance to the concept of such tampering with our nature. It seems disrespectful of the forces that created us. Beyond that, it seems frightening. We modify the behavior of plants. We control the genes of lower animals. We adapt *things* to our uses. The idea of modifying, controlling and adapting ourselves for our own purposes seems to trivialize the nature of the self. But while there may be real dangers inherent in such action, there is also danger in encouraging antitechnological prejudice.

"The Frankenstein factor"[5] is a term I have used to allude to our tendency to disproportionately distrust high-tech changes in human behavior. We do not want psychosurgery, electrode implantation or psychotropic drugs used on us or our children. Yet the mechanisms of these are not essentially different from some mechanisms we find perfectly acceptable. We may argue that they bypass normal reasoning power, and indeed they do, but so does operant conditioning, and yet most of us favor a reward system for inculcating good behavior in children. We do not teach children to become moral agents by lecturing to them or giving them texts on ethical behavior. When we try to, we realize how ineffectual it is. We teach our children through example, through role models and through reward systems, all of which bypass reasoning.

This bias against the use of nonsensory inputs is manifest in many contexts. The Hastings Center once examined the political furor caused by research in the direct control of violent behavior by the utilization of electrodes implanted in the brain or by psychosurgery—"operating on the mind."[6] The distinctions between these methods and other, less technological means were examined in order to determine to what degree the anxiety and rage were justified by the dangers and uniqueness of the procedures or were in some part an irrational response to the technology. Certainly it was ill advised, and frightening, when the surgical pioneers in this area advertised (falsely) that their research on psychosurgery for temporal-lobe epilepsy might help solve the problem of rioting in the ghettos. Temporal-lobe epilepsy is a rare and esoteric phenomenon unlikely to bring funders out of their seats with excitement. But violence in the streets was another matter, particularly at that time which followed so quickly on the riots in Detroit and Watts. It was an insensitive and foolish move for which those particular researchers were to pay a heavy price.

But realistically, it is unlikely that any authoritarian government would try to control large segments of its population by electrode implantation and psychosurgery. What emerged from that Hastings Center study was a growing concern for other, more effective means for indoctrinating large populations. The massive amount of television watching endemic with children and the movement to place children at an earlier and earlier age into school situations present two potent areas for potential political indoctrination. One essential difference between implanting an electrode and implanting an idea is that it is probably easier to remove the electrode!

Serious problems always arise when one undertakes to modify human behavior, and the problems will differ with differing methods. Whether one uses simple educational or high-tech methods, there will be anxiety about the nature of the values invariably present, if latent, in all social behavior. Whose values will prevail? How do we weigh the merits of competing values? Where is autonomy? What is the value of, and where are the limits to, variability?

To attempt radical design changes in human behavior is always dangerous. We have experienced such a radical design change not by our intentions, but through the incursion of our culture on our physiology. By developing our civilization we have invented a non-physical world. Power, passion and the struggle for survival continue. The modus vivendi and the operating rules are different, and our physiology has not caught up. Technology may have been part of the problem, but that does not preclude its being part of the solution. Whether, or when, we should pursue such attempts is a complex and confusing issue. I am not even arguing that they will ever be safe or reasonable. I see extraordinary problems in a pharmacological and physiological approach. I do not see the problem, however, in the terms that are most often offered up—the naive and mystical warnings about tampering with Mother Nature.

I have been distressed to see the amount of hysterical and wrongheaded opposition to the current research in recombinant DNA—a development in biology comparable in importance to the proposal of the germ theory by Pasteur and Koch in the nineteenth century. The potential for good in molecular biology is staggering. Of course there is potential for harm. There is in everything. Virology had frightening potential for harm, and the field has practically eliminated the great and deadly scourges of childhood. When one weighs the potential for good against the potential for bad in this procedure as one does in others, the promise in gene-splicing far outweighs the risk. But it has not been appraised like other procedures. Something else has been added: the Frankenstein factor. The procedure was beyond the understanding of the average person, and it seemed to cut to the heart of his pride in his special position as the creature created by God in His image.

While I am frightened as to how we will define improvement, who will be the deciders of the improvement and how we will measure the consequences of improvement, I am not at all intimidated by the idea of changing our species. That is our privilege. It is exclusively our privilege, granted to us by nature. In the Middle Ages Talmudists asked, "If God had intended man to be circumcised, why did he not create him so?" The answer given was that alone among creatures, man is born incomplete, with the capacity and privilege to share with his Creator in his own design. For good and for bad we have been sharing in that design for years. It is natural for us to tamper with our nature. Of course we must be as cautious and modest as we possibly can. Lessons in the past have indicated that improvements can often be fatal, but we have not, for the most part, done a bad job. Infant-mortality rates are down. [7] Children have an opportunity and expectation of living to a ripe old age. Infectious diseases in great part have been conquered. Pain can be alleviated. The deterioration of body functions can be slowed, and when they cannot, adjunctive devices (eyeglasses, hearing aids, pacemakers) can be utilized.

We *have* redesigned ourselves. Usually under the protective reassurance of the medical model. We have always felt more comfortable curing illness than improving our design. If we are infertile the corrective procedures we use to facilitate our having children (drugs, artificial insemination, *in vitro* fertilization) are medical procedures. Farsightedness is an "illness"—not the natural order of things as we really know it to be. We can correct it by filling a prescription from a physician which is paid for by our "health" insurance. This assures us that we are not committing a crime of *hubris*, we are not seeking more than our just due.

As we conquered infectious disease and arrested deteriorative conditions, we decided that we did not want the extended life expectancy if all it offered was an additional twenty years of incapacity. We wanted a greater life expectancy with a higher percentage of the attributes of youth, and we are ensuring that we get it. We have artificial supplements for hearing, for seeing, for maintaining respiration, for dialyzing our blood, for pacing our hearts. If our muscular systems are no longer as capable as they once were, no matter. We rarely use them. We are driven from place to place by automatic devices and from floor to floor by other automatic devices.

In our emotional life, we have generally felt safest when the emotions to be modified were at the extreme, such as in depression. Even then the antitechnology purists did put up resistance. The evidence is overwhelming that electric-shock treatment is no more harmful, probably less, than the prolonged use of drugs in the control of certain chronic psychiatric conditions. Yet a segment of the population in their foolishness would ban the use of shock treatment, forcing the employment of more harmful therapies.

Still, we do alter emotional states by using drugs and, in most jurisdictions, electric-shock therapy. In a more informal manner we control anxiety and "irritability" (anger) by the use of sedative drugs and tranquilizers. Valium was, for years, the most popularly dispensed drug in the United States. What is it except a means of turning off certain emotional responses that seem either inappropriate or maladaptive? It certainly is not a cure for an illness. If we have come this far with Valium I have no doubt we will go further. The immense profitability of such drugs is the ultimate spur in pharmacological research. What are the legitimate concerns we ought to face in mechanical control of anger?

One concern is that the method may be too efficient. In those things which modify behavior for adaptive purposes, we respect inefficiency. We want incremental and gradual changes that occur over extended periods of time, thus allowing for frequent evaluation and modification. The inefficiency of education has saved us from some of the wrongheaded theories of the past. Its imprecision produced a variability of response which facilitated retreat and correction when over time some of the unintended and negative results of the "improvement" became apparent.

The other major concern is in the opposite direction: the pharmacologic and surgical tools for change are still at an extraordinarily crude level. They are blunt instruments with which to attack so delicate an apparatus as human feeling. One special aspect of this is the "extraction" problem. How do we extract from the anger that we have decided is maladaptive those emotions we know to be crucial for social living? Guilt, shame and fear are still held to have strong adaptive value. Also, how could drugs distinguish those physiological responses of anger which are related to attack from those which alert for the concentrated effort of assertion?

Some problems would still remain even if we could find some way to leave the *feeling* of rage intact while separating from it those physiological aspects which are directed toward assault. This solution might be reasonable if we could find some means of instilling alternative physiological responses that would prepare us for those efforts that are effective in combating modern dangers. Certain emergencies ought to be recognized and acted upon, but the action might involve picking up a pen rather than a club. If the physiology of rage were to throw an "articulate" switch instead of a "pouncing" one, we would be better served. Our physiological mechanisms of anger ought to be operating to prepare us for who-knows-what but certainly not for direct physical assault. How can we make the adaptive response more appropriate to the real adaptive need? Unfortunately, destruction is always easier than creation. We can anticipate the capacity to ablate parts of our physiological response pattern, but it is almost impossible to even imagine the capacity for creating and installing a substitute pattern.

Another concern centers on questions of social injustice and righteous indignation. If we can believe the politicians, a truly outraged public is still the chief catalyst for political action. Anger and its public expression are a clear warning to those in authority that we mean business. Abraham Lincoln confirmed the principle that "this country, with its institutions, belongs to the people who inhabit it," continuing optimistically, "whenever they shall grow weary of the existing form of government, they may exercise their constitutional right of amending it or their revolutionary right to dismember or overthrow it."[8] I do not think any of us anticipate a revolutionary movement in this country in the foreseeable future. At least not in terms of a physical uprising overthrowing the government. But that is because our government *has* responded, often with dragging feet, to those inequities which have aroused the public ire. Inequities still exist, but the indignation they generate is still below the point of revolutionary fervor.

We must preserve the opportunity for righteous indignation. Anger must not be too cool an emotion. The feeling must generate enough heat to be uncomfortable and to force action. It must generate enough noise to be heard clearly as a warning signal to those in power. It must send out sufficient vibrations to alert and arouse those who are on the threshold of similar feelings. We ought to be offended and pained when we observe injustice and exploitation, betrayal of person or principle.

Yet I have the nagging feeling that political indignation represents only a trivial amount of the anger generated. We may generate some indignation every day over political events reported in the morning newspaper, but most of us are more likely to be angered first with our wives, children and friends, then with our colleagues and employers and then, and only then, with judges, senators and executives. What public outrage may occur is much more likely to be precipitated by crime and its consequences, or even sports. On any given day George Steinbrenner or Howard Cosell is capable of inciting more rage than Ronald Reagan. People care more about the decisions Steinbrenner makes; they "affect" their daily lives. In terms of generating the same kind of passion, unemployment, for example, tends to affect only those who are unemployed and those dependent on them. Once we are employed, our focus is turned to those areas like professional sports which may well thrive precisely because they serve to deflect our passions from areas like politics and economics which are likely to leave us feeling helpless and depressed.

Anger generated in work areas must often be contained because of fear and shame. In the home situation, anger is often contained because of love, identity and guilt. Much of this accumulated rage, like the other detritus of modern life, ends up being dumped into the streets. The deterioration of politeness and public manners is at a sufficiently rapid stage to be measurable within any one individual's experience. People rarely get up for the elderly or defer to the lame. There was a time in my memory when they did. Who cannot remember the telephone operators who were models of courtesy and patience and tact? Who does not recall the elegant and almost intimidating manners of salespersons in department stores? Modern urban life seems designed to have a coarsening and corrupting influence on human conduct. This vulgarizing process has no rationale in either logic or adaptation. Bad manners serve no purpose except to generate the same in others.

At one time we handled the deterioration of public behavior by rationalizing it. We were getting rid of old-fashioned, hypocritical forms of etiquette and decorum which were signs of a stuffy, restricted and "anal" existence. Glorying in our freedom, we decided that spontaneity meant honesty, and lack of control meant health. They mean none of these. Candor bears little relationship to honesty. It is often another form of anger. It is the closest permissible thing to a punch in the nose.

We are careful to avoid inflicting the punch in the nose which is likely to loosen the restraining bonds of fear, logic and inculcated behavior in the other person and bring a punch in the nose in return. It is interesting to observe how the hustle-bustle of the city streets is carefully choreographed to avoid all physical contact. Physical contact is a dangerous thing in the streets of the cities. Even eye contact is a dangerous phenomenon. I recall a movie review correctly criticizing as unrealistic a scene that was supposed to be taking place in New York City. The passengers in a subway train were looking at each other! No one makes eye contact in a public vehicle in New York. Certainly not in the subway. Who knows how a look may be interpreted? Who knows what it may invite? Even when bodies are jammed together during rush hour, and other people's sweat is pouring over you, eyes must be averted. The paranoid fear in the subway is so thick that even resting your eye on someone else's newspaper may be close enough to his body to be interpreted as an attack or threat. These are mean streets we are walking. And these mean streets tend to make us meaner.

I am convinced that the greatest part of anger is not produced in the service of higher goods. It is not generated by great injustices and therefore does not serve noble purposes. Even in the interpersonal relationships where expression of anger may be helpful, the massive amount generated is never completely dissipated but deflected, projected, rationalized or converted into diffuse social anger which contributes to alienation and the meanness of social life. Most anger derives from the feelings of diminution, deprivation and frustration generated out of our daily life. By our daily life I mean the nature of our work and the nature of our pleasure systems, as distinguished from any outrage at the number of children who are hungry in the Third World or other such injustices. Our humiliation is personal, but the source is usually ill defined, often unrecognizable and unknown, and therefore immune to attack.

This mass accretion of anger is dangerous because it is eminently exploitable. Anger generated by the small insults of living to which we must close our eyes will lead us to see injustice at some political level where it may not exist. We feel nobler if we think we are angry with general injustice rather than whining about our own deprivation. Of course it would be nobler to be actually fighting social injustice where it exists. This displaced anger is, however, only vaguely directed toward the political order. It is not grounded in conviction or idea. As a result, rather than being dissipated through constructive political efforts, it is usually discharged in angry rhetoric and nondirected sullenness.

The current drift into rage and cynicism cannot continue. The sociological problems are here and now, and the solutions must be found in the present if we are to salvage the future. We ought not to readjust social standards to make a greater expression of anger a tolerable norm (we cannot become Yanomamo). The potential destructive aspects of maladaptive rage might even justify physiological interventions if the physiological methods were modest and cautious. We are in no danger of overzealous interventions from this direction at the present time. An adequate technology is not at hand. We are not sophisticated enough in our knowledge to biologically modify the anger response.

Our anger is ill defined, but real. Generated by the diminutions of daily life, its mass accretion is dangerous. It cannot continue. An adequate technology is not at hand. What remains? The solution must lie in an application of knowledge derived from the psychological, sociological and political sciences. We must solve these problems by recognizing that which makes people feel threatened, and by making concerted efforts to mitigate, where possible, those forces and institutions which enrage and alienate, and where not possible, by finding compensatory rewards that enhance the pride and pleasure of the indivdual.

These problems are neither so complex, extraordinary nor unanalyzable that they resist the application of current knowledge to resolve them. We have resolved more profound problems. The dismal and unavoidable fact is that we simply have not felt the urgency. We have placed these problems low among our priorities. We had better shake up our priorities.

When the unsophisticated citizen asks how is it possible that we can find a safe way to get a man to the moon and not a safe way to walk the city streets, he is asking a reasonable question. He has a right to assume that it is the level of motivation, not the level of difficulty that leads to the failure in the latter case. We do not have at hand the prescriptive answers to the problems I have raised. That should not suggest that the problems are insoluble. They most certainly are not. If I cannot present a blueprint for what to do, I can indicate simple proved mechanisms for drafting such blueprints. The intellectual community has not applied the rigor, time and energy to these problems that they warrant. Why we have not is another sociological question that warrants some attention.

As a young psychoanalyst I became aware of the limits of my profession. Although I was enchanted with its theory and delighted with the capacity to help individuals, it became apparent to me that the number of individuals who could be helped by psychoanalysis was pitifully small. Here was a body of knowledge that ought to be useful in all forms of psychiatric treatment, and beyond that, in application to sociological problems. Otherwise psychoanalysis would seem too elegant and precious a device to warrant the enormous expense and time of training. Psychoanalysis must be placed in the service of sociological problems.

Social scientists have shamefully neglected the major problems of our time—sexism, racism, prejudice and bias, street violence, drug addiction, deterioration of the family and war. When I recently surveyed the literature on bias and prejudice I found some interesting articles on anti-Semitism and a few on racial bias, but nothing of significance on the nature of bias *per se*—on the concept of scapegoating in general. The last significant article was a thirty-year-old treatise on prejudice written by Gordon Allport.

Such neglect on the part of the intellectual community is not exactly a mystery. There are many factors involved. One is the thankless nature of approaching such work. When Kardiner and Ovesey did their basic and pioneering work on racism,[9] they were attacked as fascists. At a time when it was not yet fashionable, they declared that blacks were indeed different from whites, that they carried the "mark of oppression," and it was the price that had been paid for the so-called "separate but equal" doctrine. When Glaser and Moynihan wrote their warnings about the deterioration of the black family, they too were vilified.[10] The intellectual community did not come to their defense. Even if their ideas were incorrect, the liberal intellectual community should have supported the nature of such research. Instead, their motives were questioned and their integrity impugned.

If the danger exists of attack from within the academic community, it certainly also exists from without. Social pressure has halted major research in many areas. Research can be aborted short of picketing, boycotting or vilification. The threat of these things can put an end to the research. For a scientist the subject of research is almost always secondary to the technique. A scientist is rarely interested in cancer, schizophrenia or violence *per se*. What he is interested in is his method: tissue culture, isotope studies, analytic interviewing, cellular physiology—these technologies are his passions, the subject only his interest. He can take his expertise and apply it to a multitude of issues. The neuroanatomist concerned with plotting the way stations of the brain can be just as intrigued by problems of speech and vision as he can by problems of violence and aggression.

Violence is a good example. It is an area that ought to be researched, and I know only too well—from explicit statements made to me by department chairmen at major medical schools—that it has not been, for fear of political fallout. Faced with limited resources and limited time, there will be a natural inclination for major research departments to avoid those areas which are going to cause controversy. There are always more subjects to be examined than time allows, and scientists, like other people, will eschew those areas likely to limit their pursuits and to ensnare them in ugly personal and political controversy.

The black community, as is so often the case, has been as badly served by its friends as by its enemies. If the black family was falling apart, rather than examine what this hemorrhage might mean to the future vitality of black people, there were those in the intellectual community prepared to romanticize the patterns of absent fathers and teenage mothers as "alternative family structures"; and in the same way the concept of "black speech" romanticized the lack of education that enslaved large segments of the black population.

These issues of intellectual history are not central to the thesis being considered now. Without explicating all the aspects of our neglect of disciplined attention to the social problems of our time, we are free now to say that it must be reversed. We have a right to demand with some urgency that economists, architects, social planners, urbanologists, psychologists and sociologists begin addressing with rigor those factors which are contributing to current anomie. I repeat, these are not insoluble problems—nor, indeed, are they as difficult as others which we are in the process of solving. A species that can move easily through the field of molecular biology can certainly navigate through the problems of urban sociology. We must demand that more serious attention be paid to the factors basic to the social anger that surrounds us. When we do, the solutions will be found.

The factors that I have identified as generating fear and anger in our everyday life may constitute an incomplete list, and some may be incorrect. More important than the specifics is that the process be started. At this point I cannot offer answers but only indicate the directions in which I think the answers may be found.

Assuming some rationality and validity to the list that I have assembled, what can we do? One hardly needs a new argument to add a sense of urgency to the issue of deprived minorities. But recognizing the relationship between deprivation, bias, alienation and social anger may generate a "selfish" urgency.

We need not aspire to absolute parity in power and money; there is no evidence that such a society is feasible (although an aspiration need not be achievable to serve a useful function). We can even afford to decide that parity is not a major priority, or even a value, and yet be stable and survive. What we dare not do is disgrace or humiliate any group by defining a population of economic or power untouchables who are condemned always to be the have-nots. One need not be equal in either possessions or power to feel respectable and respected. When the disparities are too great, however, and when they seem to fall disproportionately on an ethnic or racial group, and when there is no redress, it becomes a judgment, an advertisement of contempt. This is the kind of humiliation that gnaws at self-pride and undermines self-worth. This is the alienating factor that feeds social rage, and is likely to lead to violation of social rules. Since the disadvantaged do not see themselves as part of the whole, they do not feel bound by its covenants. The majority and minority are now united in identifying two separate communities with separate loyalties, values and rules. Empathy and compassion are limited primarily to the "us," and we feel distrust for the "other." The cycle of alienation rolls on, with increasing anger being converted into antisocial behavior and distrust into paranoia. A greater sense of opportunity and equity would facilitate a reawakening of concepts of personal responsibility, and a reemergence of the right of community. If the individual does not feel a part of the community in terms of shared goods or love, it is difficult to hold him to the manners of the community or a responsibility for its well-being.

We have entered an age in which *ressentiment* is not the exclusive possession of alienated minorities—in which a majority can feel itself an alien population in its own land. The blue-collar worker feels alienated from the liberal tradition of the New Deal, which had been constructed with his needs in mind. That liberal community which romanticized Tom Joad[11] in his distress now seems to have cast him and his fellow blue-collar white Americans as the current villains. It has neglected his sensitivities. He has become less needy in terms of material goods, but no one in a society as large and impersonal as ours is ever less needy in terms of respect and community esteem. His resentment of welfare benefits for the poor is not a lack of generosity, but frustration that his "hungers" go unattended while others are "indulged." And he is angry.

Perhaps he would be less resentful of welfare if he had not seen his diligence and hard work come to naught. The greedy erosion of his savings by inflation is perceived as a betrayal. After a lifetime of sweat his pension is now a pittance. How did it happen that money that cost so much in labor when he was young buys so little in goods now that he has become old? This inflation was certainly not stoked by welfare needs; but in the minds of many resentful blue-collar workers there seems an inevitable relationship between the diminution of their security, deflation of their pride and self-esteem and the indifference and antipathy of a liberal community that seemed to have reserved all its empathy for those who "did not care enough to take care of themselves." We must reeducate the blue-collar worker, *and* attend to his miseries.

And what of work? There seems no urgency anymore to approach the question of dehumanizing work. Perhaps in periods of unemployment any job is acceptable. Twenty or thirty years ago, people of responsibility in the socioeconomic areas of academia were raising questions about the thirty-hour week, the enhanced use of leisure time and alienation in the workplace. Maybe our economic realities are different and we can no longer afford a thirty-hour week. But certainly some enlightened thinking ought to be going on at this time about how robotlike work can be converted into tolerability at least. Perhaps we cannot restore satisfaction in work, but can we not at least keep it from being totally dehumanizing? And if we cannot, is there some other method of ensuring that the worker can identify, if not with the specific work of his hands, at least with the product of the communal effort?

We can never return to the time of the small farm and the individual artisan. Our economy will continue to be industrialized and offer little opportunity for individual creativity. But the singer in the chorus takes pride in his participation, knowing that the glorious music emerging is partly his. Can there not be some way to establish a community identity in work? The Japanese seem to have done somewhat better than we have. It is impossible to make comparisons across cultures as different as ours is from the Japanese. Individual pleasure was never a central aspiration in Japan. Duty outranks pleasure in the Japanese hierarchy of motivational forces. Perhaps equivalent aspects of the American character can be identified that will endow work with pride. Pride is a bulwark of that self-esteem which defends against the anger of frustration and humiliation.

Something also must be done to help reestablish the meaning of community in terms that can be encompassed by the average human being. I am a different person in my hometown of nine thousand people than I am in my work town of sixteen million. I am less likely there to make public displays of anger because I know everyone in my town—not literally, of course, but in my feelings. The person at whom I rudely honk may well be my next-door neighbor or, worse, the plumber on whom I am so desperately dependent and whose goodwill is much more necessary for my survival than the three minutes by which he is delaying me at the crossroads.

A sense of community at one time existed in New York. "Harlem," "Washington Heights," "the Lower East Side," "Bensonhurst," "Yorkville," "Gramercy Park," "Mosholu Parkway," "the Concourse" and "Flatbush" identified specific communities with clear-cut cultural characteristics, not just geographical boundaries. You knew where to go for a real Jewish deli, a good German pastry shop, an authentic Irish bar. Of course, the neighborhood communities still exist to an extent, but there has been a real erosion. Some of that erosion is a sign of progress, marking a breakdown of ethnocentricity. But even when the concentration was rooted in anxiety, those communities offered a set of people within a specific locale who shared a sense of common purpose and identity. Much of the sense of community was centered around the public school. Children attended the neighborhood school, and the school helped define the neighborhood. The rise of private schools in the urban centers, either as a response to affluence or as a resistance to desegregation, has made the community a thinner place. It is one thing that has contributed to reducing the meaning of neighborhood into geographic location. Every solution we seek seems to compound our problems. The busing that was going to enforce desegregation has been inflammatory and has further undermined the sense of place, roots and community.

Harry Crews, the novelist, describes searching for his past in memories of his father:

Some men were sitting around in the back of the store on nail kegs or ladder-back chairs, squatting on their heels, apparently doing nothing very much but smoking and chewing and talking. . . .

We hadn't been there long before Uncle Alton said casually, as though it were something that had just occurred to him: "This is Ray Crews' boy. Named Harry."

The men turned and looked at me for a long considered time and it again seemed the most natural thing in the world for them to now begin talking about my Daddy, who had been dead for more than twenty years. . . .

Listening to them talk, I wondered what would give credibility to my own story if, when my young son grows to manhood, he has to go looking for me in the mouths and memories of other people. Who would tell the stories? . . . They are scattered all over the country, but even if he could find them, they would speak to him with no shared voice from no common ground. Even as I was gladdened listening to the stories of my Daddy, an almost nauseous sadness settled in me, knowing I would leave no such life intact. Among the men with whom I have spent my working life, University professors, there is not one friend of the sort I was listening to speak of my Daddy there that day in the back of the store in Bacon County. Acquaintances, but no friends. For half of my life I have been in the University, but never of it. Never *of* anywhere. Except the place I left, and that of necessity only in memory. [12]

The desire for community is so great that even when minimal opportunities are afforded we grasp at them. In the safe, stratified areas of the Upper East Side, people form fealties, attachments and devotion to their block. I have heard friends complain of how they miss the old neighborhood when they have moved from East 79th to East 72nd Street. The vertical nature of New York City defines space in three dimensions, as distinguished from other towns that have a mere two-dimensional concept of living. If there are fifty people to a block and it takes one thousand people to support a luncheonette, a cleaning store, a cobbler, a grocer, there will be one of these every twenty blocks. If there are a thousand people in a block one will have one of each of these in each block. New Yorkers have shown their need for community by their capacity for allegiance. They like walking into the same luncheonette every morning, having the same counterman serve them, unordered, the same coffee-black-with-buttered-bran. There they find the security of belonging, of being in the right place, and a pride in recognition. It is in every way the equivalent of the elaborate fandango of the maître d' at the fashionable French restaurant on recognizing a preferred customer. Where are the creative ideas and imaginative planning by architects and urban specialists (which Jane Jacobs called for so long ago) that would indicate their acknowledgment of the importance of neighborhood? Local neighborhoods, by allowing people to feel they can belong to something, would allow them to feel they could belong to something larger, thus supporting the legal neighborhood that is called a city. Belonging establishes kinship and security. It alleviates the sense of estrangement and isolation that, by accentuating our vulnerability, generates the fear and rage with which we are biologically equipped to greet the stranger.

Nowadays the only time that one has a real sense of community is with a great victory—winning the World Series—or a great disaster. There is no more delightful place than a major city during a crippling snowstorm. Even a blackout, except for the dangers it presents because of the marauders and looters who see in every tragedy an opportunity for self-improvement, brings out a hidden charm in city dwellers. People actually begin to talk to each other. In snowstorms the same person who might risk a pedestrian's life if he had not made it across the avenue with the light might even stop to offer a lift. When we are all suffering we are all equal. There is neither privileged nor deprived, predator nor prey. Must there be a sense of suffering for us to rediscover our humanity?

Identification destroys barriers. My children are myself. Hurt them and you hurt me. I have brown eyes. My children have blue eyes. We do not identify eye color as a boundary characteristic. If skin color were a homozygous trait and black and white were distributed throughout our children like eye-color variations, it would have precisely the same minimal significance. I am not optimistic about the possibility of dismantling cross-racial barriers in the near future. I do not look for solutions to near-range problems through the perfectibility of the species.

Fortunately, we do not have to. We know enough at this point of the nature of prejudice to know that it thrives not on differences, but on the need for scapegoats. Wide differences in body form and character structure go unnoticed. More important, massive differences in station and material wealth can be tolerated as long as there is a sense of ample goods, ample services and space, and a fair opportunity for access to them in an abundant society. It is poverty combined with frustration, deprivation, humiliation and a sense of injustice that makes us require differences. We identify significant differences only as we need them.

I am aware that there is a generation of bigots, *and* some victims, who are beyond redemption. Sociological problems are always identified in the present to be resolved in the future. That always leaves a generation who are beyond reform or redemption, and from whom we must protect ourselves via controls.

This confusion about present and future is one that has plagued the discussion of crime and punishment. Recognition of the cause of crime as sociological is not going to help in dealing with the present criminals. The debate that rages about control and containment of crime is a specious one. Both sides of this debate are right, as they are both wrong. They are talking about different problems. Of course punishment is not going to solve the crime problem in the long run. We must humanistically pursue an understanding of the pathway from deprivation to resentment to antisocial behavior. A more profound dynamic in this day is the progression of the illegitimate and fatherless child, deprived of love and authority, descending beyond alienation into psychopathy and paranoia.

But for current crime we *do* need punishment. We need it to serve a common sense of justice. We need it to do service to the autonomy of the criminal. We need it to protect society. We need it because it does deter, despite all cant to the opposite. Visualize, if you can, a society under law in which there were no punishments prescribed for breaking the law.

We must recognize how communitarian a creature we are, and must seek more of our gratifications from, and devote more of our energies to, the common good. It is amazing that with all our knowledge of the empowering, ennobling feeling of giving and service, we have found so little opportunity in our social and economic and political order to exploit both the public and the private good that comes from working for a community goal in a community spirit.

A community is more than an aggregate of individuals, and human beings are never truly individual. Aristotle has told us as much. The plea here for limits to individualism is not from a political but from a biological bias. It stems from the conviction that renewed attention to community will enhance individual autonomy.

We do vest a sense of worth in our sense of autonomy, but we also vest it in feeling that we have fulfilled our obligations to self, family and community. Unfortunately, our biological sense of the "us" is small and our sense of the "other" large. Our culture has moved us rapidly to an expanding, even global, definition of community. There is no "other" anymore; consequently, the community to which our individual survival is bound is vast and all-inclusive. Our psychology does not allow such broad identification; and our biology is fixed in an obsolete conception of the nature of survival through force and conquest. How can we attack? Whom can we attack? We are all, in this atomic age, bound together in survival.

Finally, we must attend to those equally destructive factors arising from our values which feed our rage and discontent. We must make sure not only that our goals are achievable, but that they are ultimately satisfying. The greatest sense of despair comes not from the frustration of our desires, which can be righteously attributed to things beyond our control or responsibility, but from the sense of betrayal and hopelessness when on achieving our goals, we find they bring no joy or satisfaction. Where can we direct our anger, except at ourselves? Who is the instrument of our downfall; who the enemy? To have sacrificed the one lifetime a nonbeliever is allowed in the pursuit of false goals is an unbearably painful acknowledgment. We have been selling our birthright for a mess of glitzy pottage. We must rediscover the joy of constancy, devotion, loving, duty and responsibility.

We dominate and control this planet that we share with myriads of other creatures. We have vanquished enemies of greater strength and greater number. We now have nothing to fear but ourselves. Our biology has taken us far. But part of that biological nature is discordant with the culture we have created. Our anger mechanism is designed to protect us from danger derived from others. Anger arms us for the physical assault that does not come, from physical enemies that no longer exist. It prepares us for a world that we have long since ceased to occupy. In so doing, anger sends us false messages that waste our energies and distract our concentration from the real threats of modern existence. We are now threatened by the very products of that civilization which protects us from the physical terrors of the caves and jungles from which we have ascended.

We are close to the time when we will be able to redesign ourselves biologically to exclude the traditional anger responses. But we have learned to respect our design, and to distrust the permanence of our social institutions. We may yet be forced to return to those caves, at least those of us who survive, and we cannot afford to ablate rage centers which may one day be necessary to re-create a civilization.

Still, the accretion of anger continues. And it too endangers us. We are past the point of seeing the solution in either containment or discharge of the emotion. Its accretion is the central problem. Beyond threatening our existence, anger corrodes the pleasure which lends value to that existence and purpose to our survival. Caught in this biological bind, we must free ourselves by the proper utilization of those other aspects of our biology: our intelligence, our imagination, our adaptability, our courage, our perceptions, our creativity. These qualities which can save us are, not by accident, the same ones that define our humanity.

The survival of the species now depends on the development of an environment of hope. We must contain the rage within us by altering the only variables we can. If we cannot adequately change our physiology, then we must modify our culture. We must reverse the process of frustration and despair. We must no longer tolerate the gradual erosion of the public space, the diminution of our self-pride and the deterioration of mutual relationships of trust. We must resist the angry retreat to selfishness and the abandonment of ambitious dreams.

190

9. Epilogue: The Imperfectibility of (One) Man

He was five years old at the time, and I, of course, was considerably older. We were standing in the shallow end of the swimming pool and the incident that occurred was as ordinary as the casual conversations that preceded it. And yet it haunts my dreams to this day, and I suspect will continue to do so to the end of my life.

I had seen this first grandchild of mine within hours of his birth and with that seeing knew, not just understood, the meaning of biological imprinting. His image coursed through me like some secret message to an internal computer, readjusting all the patterns of my consciousness. To the lifetime of experiences that had shaped my characteristic perceptions and behavior, a new experience had been added of such magnitude that a new sensibility existed. I knew that from that time on that image was unshakably within me —no, a part of me—and in some way that I did not understand would inevitably alter, in some way I could not predict, all my awarenesses and all my judgments.

None of this was thought out. Something had changed, and I was instantly aware of that without having any inkling of what had changed. I suppose the closest thing would be its antithesis. After a shared lifetime with a spouse, at the moment of her death one must feel, beyond mere grief over the loss of a companion, a sense

191

of oneself suddenly incomplete, bereft of some vital part. Something would seem torn away; a ragged edge would be left, a wound, and all things forever would be different after that. So too was this. Except here something had been added and an almost painful sense of fullness was present. A sense of "too much" that made me seem stretched to the limits of sensitivity and more vulnerable. I tried to remember if I had experienced this with the birth of my children, one the mother of this grandchild. I could not recall. Perhaps I had, or perhaps a grandchild produces a different response because it inevitably occurs after that point when one becomes as occupied with one's past as with one's future. That tilt point must indicate the arrival of one's first acceptance of a limited future. When my children were born, the future was forever.

The love for a grandchild is an extraordinary and exceptional thing. I have seen it repeated now, blessedly, with my two granddaughters. A loving relationship totally free of guilt exists only in this special condition. Surely there is guilt with husband, wife, lover, children, parents, even friends. With grandchildren the freedom from direct responsibility, abetted by the privilege of focusing and selecting our times of involvement, allows for that rarest of phenomena—an unsullied, unambivalent love.

Somehow or other the relationships with my granddaughters are easier. I have raised two daughters, no sons. My granddaughters are so compatible with the environment of my emotions. They fit in so well. They fit in almost too well. Constant confusion was almost immediate. The names and identities were jumbled. The time frame was blurred; was it my daughter or her daughter with whom I did that, for whom I felt this? After a while it did not matter. As in watching an impressionistic movie, I learned to enjoy the confusion by simply experiencing it. The give-and-take was so natural, so graceful and so comfortable.

Why is it so different with my grandson? Perhaps it is the gender. I am faced for the first time with the difficulties my wife must have experienced in raising girls. The terrible confusion of identities. The temptation to see the child too much as an extension of the self. Time gets confused with my grandson too, but in a different way. It is now the world not of impressionism, but of surrealism. He is a serious boy and I am a frivolous and sometimes foolish person. My father was a serious man, and I find myself now relating to my grandson in the same way I related to my father! He is annoyed, as my father was, when I want to change the rules and not take the "game" seriously. If I am to be Darth Vader I must remain Darth Vader and not make silly lapses and retreats inconsistent with the scenario. But like my father he tolerates my whimsy, albeit disapprovingly, and sometimes I can even cajole him into an act of foolishness. Whatever the reason, there is always something more complicated, more mysterious in our relationship. At any rate, something like the event that happened could have happened —probably did happen—with my granddaughters on half a dozen or more occasions and passed unnoticed into troubleless history.

We were standing in the shallow end of the pool. There was some reason, I suspect, that I did not want to be in the pool; but I was entering more out of a sense of obligation or duty. He was standing near me and lightly splashing me with the cold water. His mother had cautioned him a few times not to splash, and of course he continued—at least with me, where all rules are privately negotiated and almost anything is acceptable. The water was cold. I was timid, slow in plunging into the water, and he continued to splash me teasingly.

It was an unpleasant experience, but hardly provocative. I told him gently that I thought that his mother was right, that people do not like to be splashed, that I didn't think *he* would like to be splashed. He insisted he *would* like it and he splashed me once again, continuing to say, "I would like it." At that point I became angry and said, "If you would like it, how do you like this?" Cupping my hands, I agitated the water furiously, dousing him repeatedly with waves of water.

He is a cautious child and had just begun to overcome his anxiety about the water and to enjoy it; he was unprepared for this flooding of his face. He is not a stoic child. He cries when he is hurt. He did not cry. He stared at me with a look of such bewilderment that it broke my heart. You see, I had never, to my knowledge, never—I mean never—been angry with this boy. I do not mean angry in action. I mean angry even in feeling. Nothing he had ever done had tested my patience or tried my love. No piece of behavior, as obstreperous, willful or defiant as it might have seemed to others, had evoked anything besides compassion, pain for his pain, anxiety and renewed love. He could provoke his parents and others around him, but it had never occurred to me, ever, that I could feel anger toward this child. And here, over such a trivial incident, I had lashed out with real anger—and he had recognized it.

He stood there almost immobilized. Immediately I felt a despair, a shame, a grief over my behavior inordinate to what had been done. I uttered quick apologies and reached for him. He pulled away and cried for the first time. He left the pool and stood apart, isolated from the group. I was heartsick. He would not rejoin us. My repeated apologies and requests that we make up were greeted with his announcement, his chilling announcement, "I never make up."

Of course we made up; but something had happened and something had changed. I had lost something precious. No, it was not just loss I was experiencing, it was the sickening feeling that I had willfully destroyed something irreplaceable. I had a dream that night about the incident which, with the characteristic exaggeration of the unconscious, caused such pain that it produced tears in the night. I could not remember when that had last happened. I dream about this incident perhaps once a month, perhaps somewhat less.

Eventually I became annoyed and intrigued by my own neurotic responses and have attempted the kind of analysis I might do with a patient. What was it that I thought had been destroyed? At first I felt it was that I had tarnished and stained his image of me. The adulation of a child for a grandparent can at times approximate the flow in the other direction. Never again, I felt, would he see me in quite the same way. No longer would he trust my love. I began to realize how ridiculous this was. With all his love for me, he loves his mother and father more, albeit differently. He is constantly being reprimanded by them. Anger flows freely between them in both directions and only supports the relationship by proving its durability. Besides, I have seen no difference in his behavior toward me. He still sees me as his ally and companion.

A narcissistic injury had been received but of a different sort. It was not his view of me that had changed, but rather my view of myself. Very few things that we achieve in this life ever completely satisfy us. There are very few sources of unalloyed pride, and most of us do not anymore even aspire to a state of grace. I have never been sympathetic to the Christian model. It sets too high a goal. The all-loving, all-forgiving quality of the Christian ideal seems ever more remote; yet I think that I may have seen myself, in this relationship, as having transcended my inner selfishness, my vanities, all those lesser parts of self that are daily confronted. I think I may have seen myself in this relationship not as having done something absolutely right, but as having been privileged to be a participant in something that was absolutely right. To have destroyed this rare and precious thing, to have done so over such an unaccountable and trivial provocation was to come face to face with my limitations.

Whatever other sources contributed to my anger, forcing it to spill over that threshold which I arrogantly assumed could never be breached, will never be known. But I do now know that, for me at least, there will always be anger and that I can never again trust, even under optimal conditions, that I will not behave irrationally and, if not cruelly, at least unkindly.

The rage that is within belongs to the beast that once was. It is not nature's fault that by having created civilization we disrupted the slow and elegant process of evolution. What future adaptations may yet occur will not evolve by nature, but will be engineered by ourselves. We may be forced to experiment with changing our natures directly and run the risk of unwittingly disturbing a fundamental biological system that supports our survival. It would seem prudent to begin by altering our natures indirectly through modifications of the environment which helps to shape that nature.

If the control of anger is indeed impossible then we must augment our control systems and alter our environs to minimize the insecurity from which most anger arises. We are in a situation of some danger. Not necessarily because there has been a terrible crescendo of anger in modern times, although it is my assumption that factors involved in urban society have raised the level, but more important, because the means of expressing anger have been augmented by the methods of delivery. No more will it be a fist crashing against a cheek. It may be an atomic holocaust, which will take civilization on an irrevocably downhill course, or destroy it.

Freud, in his dying years, filled with pain and pessimism, embraced the concept of love as man's hope.[1] It is ironic that this man who dealt with the nature of love so pitifully little in the body of his work should have embraced it, at the end of his life, as man's salvation. It was not a happy solution that Freud visualized. He recognized that love enhances pain as it does pleasure, but in an existential world, where life is the end, not a means, only love can lend it dignity and meaning.

Freud is quoted as having said that in this life love and work are all.[2] Freud used words in a broad and general way. Those of us familiar with his syntax know that by love he means all attachments and identifications, all relationships one with another. By work he means more than just the way one earns a living. He means mastery, pride in oneself, achievement. When he sees our salvation as through love, I choose to think that Freud means we must extend the nature and the extent of our attachments.

We must enlarge the population with which we identify. In this way the population of the "others" becomes progressively smaller as the population of the "us" expands. In doing so we magnify ourselves, and reduce our sense of vulnerability. Perhaps in the process we can overcome some of the rage that is mounting within us. We will domesticate the beast within and ensure at least a somewhat longer life for that animal form which, with all its faults, is the highest achievement of nature.

NOTES

Chapter 1

1. A poignant picture of the tensions in small-town communities is presented in Peter Davis, *Hometown*, New York: Touchstone Press, 1983.

Chapter 2

1. For a fuller discussion of the adaptive value of emotions, see Willard Gaylin, *Feelings: Our Vital Signs*, New York: Harper and Row, 1979.

2. The best discussion for the layman of Darwin's theories remains Gaylord Simpson's *The Meaning of Evolution*, New York: Mentor Books (The New American Library), 1950.

3. Walter B. Cannon, *Bodily Changes in Panic, Hunger, Fear, and Rage*, New York: Appleton Century, 1915. A readable summary for the general public of the basic theory is W. B. Cannon, *The Wisdom of the Body*, New York: Norton, 1963.

4. There is a delightful essay on "The Uniqueness of Man" in Julian Huxley, *Man in the Modern World*, New York: Mentor Books (The New American Library), 1944.

5. Theodosius Dobzhansky, *Mankind Evolving*, New Haven, Conn.: Yale University Press, 1965, is the seminal work in delineating the interplay between culture and genes in the evolution of human nature and behavior.

Chapter 3

1. This concept of "emergency emotions" and their role in mediating behavior was a central thesis of that great psychoanalytic teacher Sandor Rado. See his *Psychoanalysis of Behavior,* New York: Grune & Stratton, 1956.

2. The importance of dependency in shaping human behavior is the central thesis of Willard Gaylin, *Caring,* New York: Knopf, 1976.

3. Melanie Klein, *Contributions to Psychoanalysis,* London: Hogarth Press, 1948.

4. The best introductory works are Sigmund Freud, *A General Introduction to Psychoanalysis,* New York: Garden City Publishing, 1943, and *The Basic Writings of Sigmund Freud,* New York: The Modern Library, 1935.

5. Willard Gaylin *et al., Doing Good: The Limits of Benevolence,* New York: Pantheon, 1978.

6. John Dollard *et al., Frustration and Aggression,* New Haven, Conn.: Yale University Press, 1967.

7. This is an unreported study.

Chapter 4

1. Sigmund Freud, *Anxiety,* Lecture XXV, Standard Edition, London: Hogarth Press, Vol. XVI, p. 393.

2. For the autonomic aspects see A. F. Ax, "The Physical Differentiation Between Fear and Anger in Humans," *Psychosomatic Medicine,* 15:433–42, 1953.

3. For central-nervous-system aspects see K. E. Moyer, "The Physiology of Aggression and the Implications for Aggression Control," pp. 233–62, and "Kinds of Aggression and Their Physiological Basis," pp. 3–26, in *The Physiology of Aggression and Implications for Control,* New York: Raven Press, 1976.

4. For cognitive aspects see A. Bandura, *Aggression: A Social Learning Analysis,* Englewood Cliffs, N.J.: Prentice-Hall, 1973, and S. Schachter, "The Interaction of Cognitive and Physiological Determinants of Emotional State," in *Anxiety and Behavior,* C. D. Spielberger, ed., New York: Academic Press, 1966, pp. 193–224.

5. David Hamburg *et al.,* "Anger and Depression in the Perspective of Behavioral Biology," in *Emotions: Their Parameters and Measurement,* L. Levi, ed., New York: Raven Press, 1975, p. 239.

6. Ernest Becker, as quoted in *ibid.,* p. 167.

7. A good review of the early exploratory research in neurophysiology can be found in Magda Arnold, *Emotions and Personality,* New York: Columbia University Press, 1960.

8. J. W. Papez, "A Proposed Mechanism of Emotion," in *Basic Readings in Neuropsychology,* R. L. Isaacson, ed., New York: Harper and Row, 1964.

9. P. MacLean, "Psychosomatic Disease and the Visceral Brain: Recent Developments Bearing on the Papez Theory of Emotion," *ibid.*

10. K. Pribram and L. Kruger, "Functions of the 'Olfactory Brain,' " *ibid.*

11. Walter Freeman and James Watts, *Psychosurgery,* Springfield, Ill.: Charles C. Thomas, 1942.

12. K. E. Moyer, *op. cit.* Also M. B. Arnold, "An Excitatory Theory of Emotion," in *Feelings and Emotions: The Mooseheart Symposium,* New York: McGraw Hill, 1950, pp. 11–33.

13. For the action of frustration on anger see A. Bandura, *op. cit.* For the influence of sexual arousal see S. Antelman and R. Caggiula, "Stress-Induced Behavior: Chemotherapy Without Drugs," in *The Psychobiology of Consciousness,* J. Davidson and R. Davidson, eds., New York: Plenum, 1980, pp. 65–104. For hunger see J. P. Scott and E. Fredericson, "The Causes of Fighting in Mice and Rats," *Physiological Zoology,* 24:273–309, 1951. For fatigue see C. N. Cofer and M. H. Appley, *Motivation Theory and Research,* New York: Wiley, 1964. For overcrowding see L. Valzelli, *The Psychobiology of Aggression and Violence,* New York: Raven Press, 1981.

14. The book that generated the most controversy was Vernon Mark and Frank Ervin, *Violence and the Brain,* New York: Harper and Row, 1970.

15. A discussion of the political impact of the psychosurgery conflict can be found in Willard Gaylin *et al., Operating on the Mind,* New York: Basic Books, 1975.

16. Probably the best general summary of the biochemistry of aggression is in L. Valzelli, *op. cit.*

17. For advocates of specificity see in the bibliography Wolf and Wolff, 1947; Ax, 1953; Funkenstein, 1953; and Arnold, 1950. For arguments against specificity see Schachter and Singer, 1967, and Moyer, 1976.

18. T. Dobzhansky, *Mankind Evolving,* New Haven, Conn.: Yale University Press, 1965.

19. W. Gaylin, *In the Service of Their Country: War Resisters in Prison,* New York: Viking, 1970.

20. Freud's discovery of the signaling aspects of anxiety is presented

in his critical study S. Freud, *Inhibitions, Symptoms and Anxiety,* London: Hogarth Press, 1949.

21. This literature is reviewed in W. Gaylin, *Caring,* New York: Knopf, 1976.

22. As quoted in W. Gaylin, *Feelings: Our Vital Signs,* New York: Harper and Row, 1979, p. 43.

23. *Ibid.,* p. 52.

24. Aristotle, *Rhetoric,* Book II, Chapter 6.

Chapter 5

1. For an excellent review of Platonic and Aristotelian attitudes toward emotions see H. N. Gardiner, "The Psychology of the Affections in Plato and Aristotle," *Philosophical Review,* Vol. 28, 1919, pp. 1–26.

2. Aristotle, *Nicomachean Ethics,* Book IV, Chapter 5.

3. Seneca, *De Ira* I, IV.3–VI.1 (p. 119).

4. *Ibid.,* I, VII.1–VIII.1 (p. 125).

5. *Ibid.,* I, XVIII.6–XIX.4 (p. 157).

6. *Ibid.,* I, XVII.5–XVIII.2 (p. 153).

7. This discussion is developed in Margaret Petritz, "The Philosophy of Anger and the Virtues," *Catholic University of America Philosophical Studies,* Vol. 146, 1953.

8. Alexander Bain, *Mental Science,* New York: D. Appleton & Co., 1888, Book III, Chapter VIII.

9. A. Riboat, *The Psychology of Emotions,* New York: Charles Scribner, 1911, Part II, Chapter III.

10. Francis Richardson, *The Psychology of Pedagogy and Anger,* Baltimore: Warwick & York, 1918, p. 84.

11. *Ibid.,* p. 89

12. G. M. Stratton, *Anger, Its Religious and Moral Significance,* New York: Macmillan, 1912, p. 35.

13. *Ibid.,* p. 49.

14. *Ibid.,* p. 70.

15. *Ibid.,* p. 257.

16. *Ibid.,* p. 258.

17. *Ibid.,* p. 267.

18. Horace Fletcher, *Menticulture, the A.B.C.'s of True Living,* New York: Herbert S. Stone, 1899, pp. 13–14.

19. *Ibid.,* p. 16.

20. S. Freud: *Gradiva* (1906), Standard Edition, Vol. 9:48, London: Hogarth Press, 1955.

21. Breuer and Freud: *Studies in Hysteria* (1895), Standard Edition, London: Hogarth Press, 1955, Vol. 2, p. 1.

22. Claude Bernard (1813–78), the brilliant investigative physiologist, is generally considered the founder of modern experimental medicine.

23. P. Sterling and J. Eyer, "Biological Basis of Stress-related Mortality," *Social Science Med.*, 15: 3–42, 1981.

24. Franz Alexander, *Psychosomatic Medicine: Its Principles and Application*, New York: W. W. Norton, 1950, p. 51.

25. S. Wolf and H. H. Wolff, *Human Gastric Function*, New York: Oxford University Press, 1947.

26. For a good review see Sterling and Eyer, *op. cit.*, p. 17.

27. *Ibid.*, p. 19.

28. *Ibid.*, pp. 20–21.

29. D. A. Hamburg *et al.*, "Anger and Depression in Perspective of Behavioral Biology," in *Society, Stress and Disease*, II: *Childhood and Society*, L. Levi, ed., London: Oxford University Press, 1973, p. 270.

30. Sterling and Eyer, *op. cit.*, p. 28.

31. D. Hamburg, *op. cit.*, p. 270.

32. W. D. Gentry, A. P. Chesney *et al.*, "Effects of Anger Expression/Inhibition and Guilt on Elevated Diastolic Blood Pressure in High/Low Stress and Black/White Females," *Proceedings of the American Psychiatric Association*, 115, 1973, p. 200.

33. Sterling and Eyer, *op. cit.*, p. 23.

34. This work was pioneered by Dr. Redford B. Williams, Duke University Medical Center. The two most recent studies reported are Richard Shekelle *et al.* in *Psychosomatic Medicine*, 45:109–14, 1983, and John Barefoot *et al.*, *ibid.*, 45:59–63.

Chapter 6

1. Willard Gaylin, *The Killing of Bonnie Garland*, New York: Simon and Schuster, 1982.

2. Jean-Paul Sartre, *Anti-Semite and Jew*, New York: Schocken Books, 1948, p. 13.

3. Marie Jahoda, "Race Relations and Mental Health," in *UNESCO: The Race Question in Modern Science*, New York: Columbia University Press, 1961, p. 64.

4. Gordon Allport, *The Nature of Prejudice*, New York: Addison-Wesley, 1954, p. 9.

5. *Ibid.*, p. 25.

6. Karl Abraham, *Selected Papers of Karl Abraham,* London: Hogarth Press, 1927, pp. 137–56. The paper on depression was published in 1911.

7. Retroflexed rage is a concept introduced by Sandor Rado to explain the self-accusatory, self-deprecating behavior of depressed patients. See Rado, "Psychodynamics of Depression from the Etiologic Point of View," *Psychosomatic Medicine,* 13 (1951), pp. 51*ff.*

8. This was quoted from Leo Madow, *Anger,* New York: Charles Scribner & Sons, 1972, p. 60.

9. W. Gaylin, *The Meaning of Despair,* New York: Jason Aronson, 1968.

10. Carol Gilligan, *In a Different Voice,* Cambridge, Mass.: Harvard University Press, 1982.

11. Pico della Mirandola, "Oration on the Dignity of Man," as quoted in Ernst Cassirer *et al., The Renaissance Philosophy of Man,* Chicago: University of Chicago Press, 1956, p. 215.

Chapter 7

1. As quoted by Lori Ann Walker, *New York Times,* February 2, 1984, p. C-1.

2. This quote from Alan Stone, *Law, Psychiatry, and Morality: Essays and Analysis,* published by American Psychiatric Press, refers to the study by S. Shinnar and R. Shinnar, "The Effects of the Criminal Justice System on the Control of Crime: A Quantitive Approach," *Law and Society Review,* Vol. 9 (1979).

3. Max Scheler, *Ressentiment,* New York: Schocken Books, 1972.

4. *Ibid.,* p. 48.

5. *Ibid.,* p. 50.

Chapter 8

1. Napoleon Chagnon, *Yanomamo: The Fierce People,* New York: Holt, Rinehart & Winston, 1968.

2. Derrick Denton, *The Hunger for Salt,* New York: Springer-Verlag, 1982.

3. David Hamburg *et al.,* "Anger and Depression in Perspective of Behavioral Biology," in *Emotions: Their Parameters and Measurement,* L. Levi, ed., London: Oxford University Press, 1973, p. 137.

4. *Ibid.,* p. 237.

5. Willard Gaylin, "The Frankenstein Factor," *New England Journal of Medicine,* Vol. 297, Sept. 22, 1977, p. 665.

6. W. Gaylin *et al., Violence and the Politics of Research,* New York: Plenum Press, 1981.

7. There is, of course, still room for improvement here. America now is fourteenth, in a cluster at a low end of a curve which has African countries varying from 100 to 200 deaths per 1,000 live births and Iron Curtain countries at 25 to 50. At 11.2 we are slightly better than the United Kingdom and slightly worse than Canada. Japan sets the pace at 7.7 deaths per 1,000.

8. This is an oft-quoted passage from Lincoln's touching and poetic First Inaugural Address.

9. Abram Kardiner and Lionel Ovesey, *Mark of Oppression: Explorations in the Personality of the American Negro,* Cleveland, Ohio: World Publishing Co., 1962.

10. Nathan Glazer and Daniel Moynihan, *Beyond the Melting Pot: The Negroes, Puerto Ricans, Jews, Italians and Irish of New York City,* Cambridge, Mass.: Massachusetts Institute of Technology Press, 1970.

11. Tom Joad was the struggling young Okie in John Steinbeck, *The Grapes of Wrath,* New York: Harper and Row, 1939.

12. Harry Crews, *A Childhood,* New York: Harper and Row, 1978, pp. 17–22.

Chapter 9

1. This discussion can be found in Sigmund Freud, *Civilization and Its Discontents* (1930), Standard Edition, London: Hogarth Press, 1955, Vol. 21, p. 59.

2. *"Liebe und Arbeit."* This oft-quoted phrase is attributed to Freud by Erik Erikson, but there is no verification that he actually said it. See E. Erikson, "Identity and the Life Cycle," *Psychological Issues,* 1:1, 1959, p. 96.

SELECTED BIBLIOGRAPHY

This bibliography makes no pretense at being complete. It is intended as an introductory guide to the interested reader. Because of the complexity of the subject I have subdivided it into three distinct sections. It is obvious that the placement of some books is arbitrary, since their subject matter did not clearly fall into one specific category. Occasionally, when the title of the article did not clearly indicate the content, I have introduced an explanatory note on *my* interpretation of the central thesis.

I. Psychology and Sociology

Allport, G. *The Nature of Prejudice* (New York: Addison-Wesley, 1954).

Bach, G. R., and Goldberg, H. *Creative Aggression.* (Garden City, N.Y.: Doubleday, 1974).

Bandura, A. *Aggression: A Social Learning Analysis.* (Englewood Cliffs, N.J.: Prentice-Hall, 1973).

————, Underwood, B., and Fromson, M. E. "Disinhibition of Aggression Through Diffusion of Responsibility and Dehumanization of Victims," in *Journal of Research in Personality* 9 (4), 1975, pp. 253–69. Anonymity as a regulator of aggression (anonymity reduces cognitive guilt and thus avoids "negative self-reinforcement"). Important ramifications for violence of group against group and anonymous antisocial behavior. Presented in behavioral/cognitive terms.

Becker, E. *The Birth and Death of Meaning,* 2nd ed. (New York: Free Press, 1971).

Berkowitz, L. *Aggression: A Social Psychology Analysis.* (New York: Mc-Graw-Hill, 1962).

Bernarde, T. "Women and Anger: Conflicts with Aggression in Contemporary Women," *Journal of the American Medical Women's Association* 33 (5), 1978, pp. 215–19.

Blumenthal, M. D. "Resentment and Suspicion Among American Men,"

American Journal of Psychiatry 130 (8), pp. 876–80. Found positive correlation between low socioeconomic status and suspicion/resentment. Race also a factor.

Bowlby, J. *Attachment and Loss,* Vol. 2: *Separation, Anxiety and Anger.* (London: Hogarth Press, 1973).

Brenner, C. "The Psychoanalytic Concept of Aggression," *International Journal of Psychoanalysis* 52, 1971, pp. 137–44. Claims that aggression is instinctual and can be deduced by psychoanalytic method (without help from biology).

Crabtree, J. M., and Moyer, K. E. *Bibliography of Aggressive Behavior: A Reader's Guide to the Research Literature.* (New York: Alan R. Liss, Inc., 1977).

Freud, A. "Aggression in Relation to Emotional Development; Normal and Pathological," *Journal for the Theory of Social Behavior* 3 (2), 1973. A developmental orientation.

Freud, S. *Inhibitions, Symptoms and Anxiety* (London: Hogarth Press, 1949).

————. *Civilization and Its Discontents.* Translated and edited by Strachey, J. (New York: W. W. Norton, 1964). The social consequences of the aggressive instinct.

————. *Beyond the Pleasure Principle.* Translated and edited by Strachey, J. (New York: W. W. Norton, 1966). The most clear-cut version of Freud's "death instinct" after he revised it.

Funkenstein, D. H., King, S. H., and Drollette, M. "The Experimental Evocation of Stress," *Symposium on Stress* (Washington, D.C.: Division of Medical Sciences, National Research Council and Army Serv. Grad. School, Walter Reed Army Medical Center, GPO, 1953).

————. "The Direction of Anger During a Laboratory Stress-inducing Situation," *Psychosomatic Medicine* 16 (5), 1954, pp. 404–13.

Gaylin, Willard, *Feelings: Our Vital Signs* (New York: Harper & Row, 1979).

————. *The Killing of Bonnie Garland* (New York: Simon and Schuster, 1982).

———— et al. *Violence and the Politics of Research* (New York: Plenum Press, 1981).

Geen, R. G., and Quanty, M. B. "The Catharsis of Aggression: An Evaluation of a Hypothesis," in Berkowitz, L. *Advances in Experimental Social Psychology,* Vol. 10 (New York: Academic Press, 1977). Conflicting evidence and poor correlations among psychophysiological measures of anger in studies of its cathartic value.

Gilligan, C. *In a Different Voice* (Cambridge, Mass.: Harvard University Press, 1982).

Glazer, N., and Moynihan, D. *Beyond the Melting Pot: The Negroes, Puerto Ricans, Jews, Italians and Irish of New York City* (Cambridge, Mass.: Massachusetts Institute of Technology Press, 1970).

Hamburg, D. A., *et al.* "Anger and Depression in the Perspective of Behavioral Biology," in *Emotions: Their Parameters and Measurement,* Levi, L., ed. (New York: Raven Press, 1975).

Hamburg, D. A., Adams, J. E., and Brodie, H. K. H. "Coping Behavior in Stressful Circumstances: Some Implications for Social Psychiatry," in *Further Explorations in Social Psychiatry,* Leighton, A. H., ed. (New York: Basic Books, 1975).

Hampton, P. J. "The Many Faces of Anger," *Psychology* 15 (1), 1978, pp. 34-35.

Hartmann, H., Kris, E., and Lowenstein, R. "Notes of the Theory of Aggression," in *Psychoanalytic Study of the Child,* Vol. 3–4, pp. 9–36. Describes differences between erotic and aggressive instincts, also methods of combinations and results (e.g, masochism, sadism, etc.).

Horney, Karen. "Culture and Aggression," *American Journal of Psychoanalysis* 20 (2), 1960, pp. 130–38.

Izard, C. "The Emergence of Emotion and the Development of Consciousness in Infancy," in *The Psychobiology of Consciousness,* Davidson, J., and Davidson, R., eds. (New York: Plenum Press, 1980), pp. 193–16.

Jahoda, M. "Race Relations and Mental Health," in *UNESCO: The Race Question in Modern Science* (New York: Columbia University Press 1961), p. 64.

Kardiner, A., and Ovesey, L. *Mark of Oppression: Explorations in the Personality of the American Negro* (Cleveland, Ohio: World Publishing Co., 1962).

Kemper, T. D. *A Social Interactional Theory of Emotions* (New York: John Wiley and Sons, 1978).

Klein, M. *Contributions to Psychoanalysis* (London: Hogarth Press, 1948).

Lystad, M. H. "Violence at Home," *American Journal of Orthopsychiatry* 45 (3), pp. 328–45. A review of the literature in this area with an emphasis on abnormally violent families (wife and child abuse, etc.). Some interesting theoretical notes on the causes of everyday hostility within the family.

Madow, L. *Anger* (New York: Charles Scribner & Sons, 1972).

Mark, V. H., and Ervin, F. R. *Violence and the Brain* (New York: Harper & Row, Medical Department, 1970).

Menninger, K. *Man Against Himself* (New York: Harcourt Brace and Company, 1956).

Misterlich, A. "Psychoanalysis and the Aggression of Large Groups," *International Journal of Psychoanalysis* 52, pp. 161–68. Criticizes but does not reject the theory of aggression as instinctual. Instead, adds frustration and projection to explain fantasies and subtle feelings of aggression. Also describes an interdisciplinary approach to social psychoanalysis.

Morgan, C. T., ed. *Feelings and Emotions: The Mooseheart Symposium* (New York: McGraw-Hill, 1950).

Perry, D. G., and Perry, L. C. "Effects of Anger Arousal and Competition on Aggressive Behavior," *Journal of Child Psychology and Psychiatry* 17 (2), pp. 145–49. Experimental evidence against catharsis. Increases in competition lead to increases in anger.

Plutchik, R. *The Emotions: Facts, Theories and a New Model* (New York: Random House, 1962).

Rado, S. "Psychodynamics of Depression from the Etiologic Point of View," *Psychosomatic Medicine* 13, 1951, pp. 51*ff*.

――――. *Psychoanalysis of Behavior* (New York: Grune & Stratton, 1956).

Rothenberg, A. "On Anger," *American Journal of Psychiatry* 128, 1971, pp. 86–92 and 454–60.

Sartre, J.-P. *Anti-Semite and Jew* (New York: Schocken Books, 1948).

Schachter, S., and Singer, J. E. "Cognitive, Social, and Psychologic Determinants of Emotional State," *Psychology Review* 69, 1962, pp. 379–99.

Scott, J. P. "Violence and the Disaggregated Society," *Aggressive Behavior* 1 (3), pp. 235–60. Reviews a great deal of evidence in animal societies from ants to baboons and shows the effects of disorganization on violence. Carefully and convincingly draws some parallels with humans.

Shaver, P., Schurtman, R., and Blank, T. O. "Conflict Between Firemen and Ghetto Dwellers," *Journal of Applied Social Psychology* 5 (3), pp. 240–61. Examines the causes of false alarms in New York and gives some interesting insights into the attitudes and frustrations of the urban poor.

Shotland, R. L., and Straw, M. K. "Bystander Response to an Assault: When a Man Attacks a Woman," *Journal of Personality and Social Psychology* 34 (5), pp. 990–99. Some possible reasons for our increased tolerance of public violence. Shotland and Straw blame depersonalization.

Singh, U. R., and Sowaid, M. "Role of Parental Discipline in Hostility," *Psychologia* 19 (1), pp. 29–34. Shows negative correlation between corporal punishment as a child and hostility as an adult.

Spector, P. "Population Density and Unemployment: The Effects on the Incidence of Violent Crime in America," *Criminology* 12 (4), pp. 399–401. Shows no significant correlation between population density (i.e., overcrowding) or rate of unemployment and violent crime.

———, Penner, L., and Hawkins, H. "The Effects of Thwarting Aggression on Subsequent Aggression," *Social Behavior and Personality* 3 (2), pp. 233–41. Reinforces frustration hypothesis—thwarting of goal-oriented response leads to second response which is manifested as increased aggression.

Stearns, F. R. *Anger: Psychology, Physiology, Pathology* (Springfield, Ill.: Charles C. Thomas, 1972).

Stone, A. *Law, Psychiatry and Morality* (Washington, D.C.: American Psychiatric Press, forthcoming).

Strongman, K. T. *The Psychology of Emotion* (New York: John Wiley and Sons, 1973).

Tavris, C. *Anger: The Misunderstood Emotion* (New York: Touchstone Press, 1984).

Weiss, J. M. "Psychological Factors in Stress and Disease," *Scientific American* 226, 1972, pp. 104–20.

Weiss, N. S. "Recent Trends in Violent Deaths Among Young Adults in the United States," *American Journal of Epidemiology* 103 (4), pp. 417–22. Statistically, America is becoming more violent. Suicide, homicide and accidental deaths are up dramatically, particularly among young males.

II. Biophysiology

Alexander, F. *Psychosomatic Medicine: Its Principles and Applications* (New York: W. W. Norton, 1950).

Arnold, M. B. "An Excitatory Theory of Emotion," in *Feelings and Emotions: The Mooseheart Symposium* (New York: McGraw-Hill, 1950), pp. 11–33.

———. *Emotions and Personality.* (New York: Columbia University Press, 1960).

Ax, A. F. "The Physical Differentiation Between Fear and Anger in

Humans," *Psychosomatic Medicine* 15, 1953, pp. 433–22.

Axelrod, J. "Biogenic Amines and Their Impact on Psychiatry," *Psychiatry* 4, 1972, pp. 199–210.

Barchas, J. D., Ciaranell, R. D., *et al.* "Genetic Aspects of Catecholamine Synthesis," in *Hormones and Behavior,* Levine, S., ed. (New York: Academic Press, 1972), pp. 235–319.

Barefoot, J. C., *et al.* "Hostility, CHD Incidence and Total Mortality: A 25-Year Follow-Up Study of 255 Physicians," *Psychosomatic Medicine* 45, 1983, pp. 59–63.

Bear, D. M., and Fedio, P. "Quantitative Analysis of Interictal Behavior in Temporal Lobe Epilepsy," *Archives of Neurology* 34, 1977, pp. 454–67.

Board, F., Persky, H., and Hamburg, D. A. "Psychological Stress and Endocrine Function," *Psychosomatic Medicine* 18, 1956, pp. 324–33.

Cannon, W. B. *Bodily Changes in Panic, Hunger, Fear, and Rage* (New York: Appleton-Century, 1915). A readable summary for the general public of the basic theory in Cannon, W. B., *The Wisdom of the Body* (New York: Norton Library, 1963).

———. "The James-Lange Theory of Emotion," *American Journal of Psychology* 39, pp. 106–24.

Cantril, H., and Hunt, W. A. "Emotional Effects Produced by Injection of Adrenalin," *American Journal of Psychology* 44, pp. 300–07.

Contrada, R., Glass, D., *et al.* "Effects of Control over Aversive Stimulation and Type A Behavior on Cardiovascular and Plasma Catecholamine Responses," *Psychophysiology* 19, 1982, pp. 408–19.

Davidson, J., and Davidson, R., eds. *The Psychobiology of Consciousness* (New York: Plenum Press, 1980).

Dembroski, T., *et al.* "Effects of Level of Challenge on Pressor and Heart Responses in Type A and B Subjects," *Journal of Applied Social Psychology* 9, 1979, pp. 209–28.

Eccles, J. *The Neurophysiological Basis of Mind* (Oxford: Clarendon Press, 1953).

Echelman, B., and Thoa, N. B. "The Aggressive Monoamines," *Biol. Psychiatry* 6, 1973, pp. 143–64.

Eleftheriou, B. E., and Scott, J. P., eds. *The Physiology of Aggression and Defeat* (New York: Plenum Press, 1971).

Elmadjian, J., Hope, J., and Lamson, E. T. "Excretion of Epinephrine and Norepinephrine in Various Emotional States, " *Journal of Clinical Endocrinology* 17, 1957, pp. 608–20.

Frankenhauser, M. *et al.* "Notes on Arousing Type A Persons by Depriving Them of Work," *Journal of Psychosomatic Res.* 24, 1980.

————. "Experimental Approaches to the Study of Catecholamines and Emotions," in *Emotions: Their Parameters and Measurement,* Levi, L., ed. (New York: Raven Press, 1975), pp. 209–31.

Funkenstein, D. H. "The Physiology of Fear and Anger," *Scientific American* 192, 1955, pp. 74–80.

————. "Norepinephine-like and Epinephrine-like Substances in Relation to Human Behavior," *Journal of Mental Disorders* 124, 1956, pp. 58–68.

Gentry, W. D., Chesney, A. P., *et al.* "Habitual Anger-coping Styles: I. Effect on Mean Blood Pressure and Risk for Essential Hypertension," *Psychosomatic Medicine* 44, 1982, pp. 195–202.

Gentry, W. D., Harburg, E., *et al.* "Effects of Anger Expression/Inhibition and Guilt on Elevated Diastolic Blood Pressure in High/Low Stress and Black/White Females," *Proceedings of the American Psychiatric Association* 115, 1973, p. 200.

Greenfield, N. S., and Sternbach, R. A., eds. *Handbook of Psychophysiology* (New York: Holt, Rinehart and Winston, 1972).

Grossarth-Matizek, R. "Psychosocial Predictors of Cancer and Internal Disease," *Psychotherapy and Psychosomatics* 33, 1980, pp. 122–28.

Hamburg, B. A., and Hamburg, D. A. "Stressful Transitions of Adolescence: Endocrine and Psychosocial Aspects," in *Society, Stress and Disease,* II: *Childhood and Society,* Levi, L., ed. (London: Oxford University Press, 1973), p. 270.

Hamburg, D. A. "Emotions in the Perspective of Human Evolution," in *Expression of the Emotions in Man,* Knapp, P., ed. (New York: International Universities Press, 1968), pp. 300–17.

Hinde, R. *The Biological Basis of Social Behavior* (New York: McGraw-Hill, 1974).

Ingram, W. R. *A Review of Anatomical Neurology* (Baltimore: University Park Press, 1976).

Kagan, A. "Epidemiology, Disease and Emotion," in *Emotions: Their Parameters and Measurement,* Levi, L., ed. (New York: Raven Press, 1975), pp. 531–39.

Kety, S., and Schildkraut, J. "Biogenic Amines and Emotion," *Science* 156, 1967, pp. 21–36.

Levi, L., ed. *Emotions: Their Parameters and Measurement* (New York: Raven Press, 1975).

Levitan, H. L. "Psychological Factors in the Etiology of Ulcerative Colitis," *International Journal of Psychiatry and Medicine* 7, 1977, pp. 221–28.

MacLean, P. "Psychosomatic Disease and the Visceral Brain: Recent Developments Bearing on the Papez Theory of Emotion," in *Neuropsy-chology*, Isaacson, R. L., ed. (New York: Harper and Row, 1964).

Mikhail, A. "Psychological Stress and Stomach Ulcer: In Search of an Hypothesis," *Brain Research Bulletin*, 5 Suppl., 1, 1980, pp. 67–71.

Moyer, K. E., ed. *The Physiology of Aggression and Implications for Control* (New York: Raven Press, 1976).

Novaco, R. W. "The Functions and Regulation of the Arousal of Anger," *American Journal of Psychiatry* 133, 1976, pp. 1124–27.

Papez, J. W. "A Proposed Mechanism of Emotion," in *Neuropsychology*, Isaacson, R. L., ed. (New York: Harper and Row, 1964).

Pribram, K., and Kruger, L. "Functions of the 'Olfactory Brain,' " in *Basic Readings in Neuropsychology*, Isaacson, R. L., ed. (New York: Harper and Row, 1964).

Reis, D. J. "Central Neurotransmitters in Aggression," in *Association for Research in Nervous and Mental Diseases Symposium on Aggression*, Vol. 52, Frazier, S., ed. (Baltimore: Williams and Wilkins, 1974), pp. 119–47.

Selye, H. "The General Adaption Syndrome and the Diseases of Adaptation," *Journal of Clinical Endocrinology* 6, 1946, p. 117.

Shekelle, R. B., *et al.* "Hostility, Risk of Coronary Heart Disease and Mortality," *Psychosomatic Medicine* 45, 1983, pp. 109–14.

Sigg, E. B. "The Organization and Function of the Central Nervous System," in *Emotions: Their Parameters and Measurement*, Levi, L., ed (New York: Raven Press, 1975), pp. 93-122.

Snyder, S. "Amphetamine Psychosis: A 'Model' Schizophrenia Mediated by Catecholamines," *American Journal of Psychiatry* 130, 1973, pp. 61–67.

Stearns, F. R. *Anger: Psychology, Physiology, Pathology* (Springfield, Ill.: Charles C. Thomas, 1972).

Sterling, P., and Eyer, J. "Biological Basis of Stress-related Mortality," *Social Science & Medicine* 15, 1981, pp. 3–42.

Stolk, J. M., Conner, R. L., Levine, S., *et al.* "Brain Norepinephrine and Shock-induced Fighting Behavior in Rats," *Journal of Pharmacology and Experimental Therapeutics* 190, 1974, pp. 193–209.

Taliamonte, A., *et al.* "Free Tryptophan Level and Serotonin Synthesis," *Life Sciences* 12, 1973, pp. 277–87.

Thierry, A. M., *et al.* "Selective Activation of the Mesocortical DA System by Stress," *Nature* 263, 1976, pp. 242–43.

Thoa, N. B., Eichelman, B., Richardson, J. S., *et al.* "6-hydroxydopa

Depletion of Brain Norepinephrine and the Facilitation of Aggressive Behavior," *Science* 178, 1972, pp. 75–77.

Torda, C. "Observations on the Effects of Anxiety and Anger on the Content of Concurrent Dreams," *American Journal of Clinical Hypnosis* 17, 1975, pp. 253–59.

Undenfriend, S. "Molecular Biology of the Sympathetic Nervous System," *Pharmacology Review* 24, 1972, pp. 165–66.

Valzelli, L. *The Psychobiology of Aggression and Violence* (New York: Raven Press, 1981).

Wolf, S. "Emotions and the Autonomic Nervous System," *Archives of Internal Medicine* 126, 1970, p. 1024.

———. "Regulatory Mechanisms and Tissue Pathology," in *Emotions: Their Parameters and Measurement,* Levi, L., ed. (New York: Raven Press, 1975), pp. 619–25.

———, and Wolff, H. G. *Human Gastric Function* (New York: Oxford University Press, 1943).

III. History and Anthropology

Aristotle. *Nicomachean Ethics,* translation by Oswald, M. (Indianapolis: Bobbs-Merrill Co., Inc., 1962), Book IV, Chapter 5.

Bain, A. *Mental Science: A Compendium of Psychology and the History of Philosophy* (New York: D. Appleton and Co., 1888), Book III, Chapter VIII.

Bolton, R. "Anger in Quolla Society," 1972, dissertation found on microfilm.

Booth, Sally Smith. Book review of Billings, W. M., *Seeds of Anger: Revolts in America, 1607–1771* (New York: Hastings House, 1977), *Journal of American History* 65, 1978, pp. 748–49.

Bramson, L., and Goethals, S. W., eds. *War: Studies from Psychology, Sociology, and Anthropology* (New York: Basic Books, 1964). Causes and nature of human aggression, international conflict and war. Also includes war as behavior.

Buss, A. *The Psychology of Aggression* (New York: John Wiley and Sons, Inc., 1961).

Chagnon, N. *Yanomamo: The Fierce People* (New York: Holt, Rinehart and Winston, 1968).

Fletcher, H. *Menticulture, the A.B.C.'s of True Living* (New York: Herbert S. Stone and Co., 1899).

Freeman, D. "Human Aggression in Anthropological Perspective, " in

The Natural History of Aggression, Carthy, J. D., and Ebling, F. J., eds. (New York: Academic Press, Inc., 1964).

Gardiner, H. N. "The Psychology of the Affections in Plato and Aristotle," *Philosophical Review* 28, 1919, pp. 1–26.

Gates, G. S. "An Observational Study of Anger," *Journal of Experimental Psychology* 9, 1926, pp. 325–36.

Goodenough, F. L. *Anger in Young Children* (Westport, Conn.: Greenwood Press, 1931).

Graham, H. D., and Gurr, T. R. "Violence in America: Historical and Comparative Perspectives," a report to the National Commission on the Causes and Prevention of Violence, 1969.

Gurr, T. R. "The Psychological Factors in Civil Violence," *World Politics* 20, 1968.

Hsu, F. *The Psychological Approach to Anthropology* (Homewood, Ill.: The Dorsey Press, 1961).

Hyslop, T. B. "Anger," *Journal of Mental Science* 61, 1915, pp. 371–91.

Levine, R. A. "Anthropology and the Study of Conflict," *Journal of Conflict Resolution* 5, 1961, pp. 3–15.

Nordstrom, C., *et al.* "The Influence of Ressentiment on Student Experience in Secondary School," Cooperative Research Project No. 1758, Brooklyn College, 1965.

Paddock, J. "Studies on Antiviolent and 'Normal' Communities," *Aggressive Behavior* 1 (3), pp. 217–33. A study of several towns in southern Mexico with similar geography, genetic makeup, economic level, language, etc. Some, however, control violence without formal punishment. Differences in attitudes and ethnography are examined.

Petritz, M. "The Philosophy of Anger and the Vitues," *Catholic University of America Philosophical Studies* 146, 1953.

Ribot, T. A. *The Psychology of Emotions* (New York: Charles Scribner's Sons, 1911), Part II, Chapter III.

Richardson, R. F. *The Psychology of Pedagogy and Anger* (Baltimore: Warwick and York, Inc., 1918).

Seneca. *On Anger,* Basore, J. W., trans., Moral Essays, Loeb Classical Library (Cambridge, Mass.: Harvard University Press, 1963).

Scheler, M. *Ressentiment* (New York: Schocken Books, 1972).

Stratton, G. M. *Anger: Its Religious and Moral Significance* (New York: The Macmillan Co., 1912).

Turnbull, Colin M. *The Mountain People* (New York: Touchstone Books, 1972).

INDEX

215